Getting Started with Business Analytics

Insightful Decision-Making

Getting Started with Business Analytics

Insightful Decision-Making

David Roi Hardoon and Galit Shmueli

CRC Press
Taylor & Francis Group
Boca Raton London New York

CRC Press is an imprint of the
Taylor & Francis Group, an informa business
A CHAPMAN & HALL BOOK

Reprint, 2016

CRC Press
Taylor & Francis Group
6000 Broken Sound Parkway NW, Suite 300
Boca Raton, FL 33487-2742

ISBN: 978-1-4987-8741-3

Library of Congress Cataloging-in-Publication Data

Hardoon, David Roi.
Getting started with business analytics : insightful decision-making / David Roi Hardoon, Galit Shmueli.
pages cm. -- (Chapman & Hall/CRC machine learning & pattern recognition series)
Includes bibliographical references and index.
ISBN 978-1-4398-9653-2 (hardcover : alk. paper)
1. Decision making--Statistical methods. 2. Business planning--Statistical methods. 3. Data mining. I. Shmueli, Galit, 1971- II. Title.

HD30.23.H3656 2013
658.4'033--dc23 2012050718

Visit the Taylor & Francis Web site at
http://www.taylorandfrancis.com

and the CRC Press Web site at
http://www.crcpress.com

Dedicated to
Those Who Want to Know

Contents

Foreword

This century is seeing the rise of the "data scientist," driven by the increasing convergence of data and technology. The digitization of the world has given birth to a plethora of data sources, and distilling them for insights and competitive advantages has become a fast burgeoning industry. Unfortunately, for anyone wanting to break into this field, the preparatory curriculum of the day is limited. It focuses predominantly on the theoretical (or mathematical) aspect of the technique rather than the objective of the solution, i.e., what is the business challenge that we are endeavoring to solve?

David R. Hardoon and Galit Shmueli have chosen to break away from the typical and traditional introduction to database marketing and data mining. Instead, in easily accessible language, they have approached it from the perspective of how these techniques can be applied to solve various business problems. From banking to telecommunication, from retail to health care, from transportation to manufacturing, these data mining techniques are transforming the way we optimize businesses.

This book offers an introduction to the essence of ***business analytics***, providing a good summary of the analytical solutions employed across these industries today, including an updated vocabulary on new domains such as social media. The reader will appreciate the difference between supervised and unsupervised learning, *k*-means clustering, and regression tree classification. Understanding the context in which to apply the right solution approach is often as crucial as the technical mastery of the science itself. As they say, framing the problem is half the solution.

Getting Started with Business Analytics: Insightful Decision-Making will simplify, and demystify the concepts around the "science of data." Looking back at my career in the field of business analytics, I realize that it would have been extremely helpful to have had such a book in hand. It would have provided me with guidance on structuring my analytical solutions and would have inspired me to greater creativity. I hope this book will light the spark of curiosity for a new generation of data scientists.

Eric Sandosham
Managing Director & Regional Head, Decision Management
Citibank, Asia Pacific 2010–2012

Preface

In recent years, the term *business analytics* has been promoted by software vendors, service providers, technology developers and consulting firms. These promotion efforts have focused predominantly on technological capabilities and examples of the benefits derived from using such systems.

Despite the availability of large amounts of hard data and information such as scorecards and metrics, intuition is still the basis for many important, and sometimes critical, decisions by senior executives and managers. This book will help you replace gut-feel decision-making with decisions based on hard data.

We ourselves realized that on many occasions, when business analytics was explained or presented, it was implicitly assumed that the audience had prior understanding of what business analytics is all about. Moreover, different speakers and experts seem to have different notions of what business analytics includes, excludes, and refers to. The conflation has become more problematic now that many fields and organizations have an incentive to claim business analytics as their own. Business analytics relies heavily on data mining which creates an added layer of confusion. What is business analytics? What is data mining? What is the framework that ties data mining within business analytics? There are some excellent books on business analytics[1] as well as books on data mining intended for a business audience[2]. However, there appears to be a gap when it comes to providing an integrated picture that has sufficient detail.

This situation motivated us to write a book that takes a step back and describes business analytics from a noncommercial, no-agenda standpoint. We do not assume that you know what the topic is about before you start reading. In particular, we make no assumptions about your level of knowledge or technical skill. Instead, we guide you through a journey into the world of business analytics, exploring its

[1] Thomas H. Davenport and Jeanne G. Harris. *Competing on Analytics: The New Science of Winning*. Harvard Business School Press, 2007; Thomas H. Davenport, Jeanne G. Harris, and Robert Morison. *Analytics at Work: Smarter Decisions, Better Results*. Harvard Business School Press, 2010; and Evan Stubbs. *Value of Business Analytics: Identifying the Path to Profitability*. Wiley, 2011.

[2] Galit Shmueli, Nitin R. Patel, and Peter C. Bruce. *Data Mining for Business Intelligence: Concepts, Techniques, and Applications in Microsoft Office Excel with XLMiner*. Wiley, 2010; and Colleen McCue. *Data Mining and Predictive Analysis: Intelligence Gathering and Crime Analysis*. Butterworth-Heinemann, 2007.

contents, capabilities, and applications. We try to explain and demystify the main concepts and terminologies, and give many examples of real-world applications.

We wrote the book with a diverse audience in mind: students, managers, analysts, executives, consultants and whoever may need to interact with or alongside individuals or departments deploying business analytics solutions.

This book has three parts:

Part I is a general introduction to business analytics. Chapter 1 introduces you to the world of business data and to recent technologies that have promoted fact-based decision-making. We look at "business intelligence" and how it differs from "business analytics." In Chapter 2 we discuss the main components that comprise a business analytics application and various requirements for integrating the business with the analytics.

Part II introduces you to the basics of *data mining* and *data analytics*, which are the technologies underlying business analytics. Chapter 3 is a crash course in data mining, at the end of which you will be versed in the main concepts and ideas behind these technologies. Chapter 4 shows how data mining has expanded into "data analytics" when considering new types of data such as network and text data.

Part III delves into business analytics and looks at three main areas in depth: Chapter 5 describes *customer analytics*, Chapter 6 focuses on *social analytics*, and finally Chapter 7 covers *operational analytics*. At the end of each chapter we suggest a hands-on project based on using publicly available data.

While we recommend that novices follow the natural flow above, each part can be read independently.

Acknowledgments

David would like to thank the many colleagues in industry and academia who have helped shape his understanding of analytics and its application in business. Thanks to Eric Sandosham for his instrumental support, encouragement, and in particular for a specific presentation at the National University of Singapore Business School that started his business analytics journey. Thanks to Nimish Panchmatia for igniting the love of operations and Tan Poh Choo who enabled my business analytics playing field, as well as giving feedback on an early draft of the book. Furthermore, I would like to thank Ji Jun Yao and Li Jun for providing screenshots, and Eva Phua, Evan Stubbs and Kelvin Chng for giving valuable critique at different stages of the book writing. Last but not least, Melissa, Arrielle and Ori, for their understanding of the time taken to complete this manuscript.

Galit is grateful to many colleagues in academia and industry around the globe as well as past students from the University of Maryland and the Indian School of Business who have shared their analytics experiences. Thanks to Reema Gupta from SRITNE at the Indian School of Business, who championed several industry–academia events and programs through which I was able to connect with many analytics professionals in India. Thanks to the many LinkedIn members in various analytics groups for great discussions. All these avenues have opened my mind to "known unknowns" as well as allowing me to recognize the many "unknown unknowns" in academia and in industry. Heartfelt thanks to Raquelle Azran for her meticulous reading and editing of the book. Many thanks to Peter Bruce, Ron Kenett and Kishore Rajgopal for their insightful feedback and comments on an earlier draft of the book. Last, but not least, Boaz and Noa Shmueli for their understanding of the time taken to complete this manuscript.

Both authors thank our CRC Press editor, Randi Cohen,

for her assistance in guiding the book and supporting our sometimes unusual directions.

Legal Notices

We thank Professors Gal Oestreicher-Singer and Arun Sundararajan for their permission to use the Amazon products network image, and Kishore Rajgopal and Divyabh Mishra for their permission to use the CrowdANALYTIX material.

Part I

Introduction to Business Analytics

1 *The Paradigm Shift*

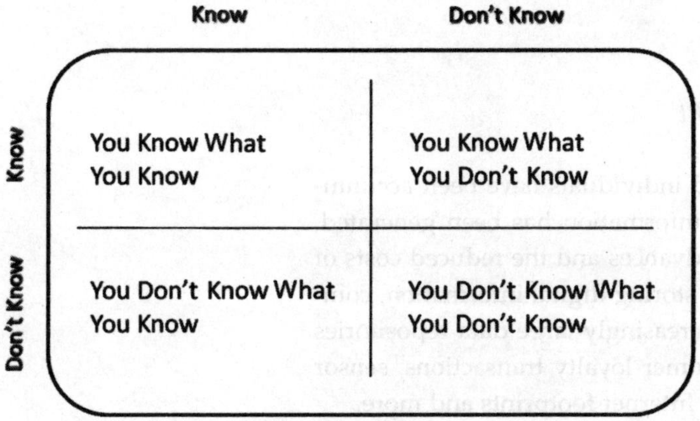

There are known knowns. These are things we know that we know. There are known unknowns. That is to say, there are things that we know we don't know. But there are also unknown unknowns. There are things we don't know we don't know.

— Donald H. Rumsfeld (1932–)
American Politician and Businessman

Despite the availability of raw information such as scorecards and metrics, intuition is still the basis for many important, and sometimes critical, decisions by senior executives and managers. The area of Business Analytics aims to alter the approach of relying on intuition alone by applying analytical techniques to data in order to create insightful and efficient resolutions to everyday business issues and to create value.

Business Analytics can be used for improving performance, driving sustainable growth through innovation, speeding up response time to market and environmental changes, and anticipating and planning for change while managing and balancing risk.

These benefits are achieved through a framework that deploys automated data analysis within the business context. The paradigm shift is from intuition-driven decision making to data-driven, computer-assisted decision making that takes advantage of large amounts of data or data from multiple sources.

1.1 *From Data to Insight*

Societies, organizations and individuals have been accumulating data for as long as information has been generated. With recent technological advances and the reduced costs of collecting, transferring and storing digital information, companies are accumulating increasingly large data repositories of emails, documents, customer loyalty transactions, sensor data, financial information, Internet footprints and more.

The fascination with data is due to the potential it holds for gaining knowledge. As cognitive psychology has shown us, not only is human memory less than perfect and human knowledge limited, but more disturbingly, we are susceptible to the *illusion of memory* and the *illusion of knowledge*[1]. We think that our memories are accurate and believe that our knowledge is correct, yet often that is not the case. See figure 1.1 for an example of optical illusions.

[1] *The Invisible Gorilla: And Other Ways Our Intuitions Deceive Us* by Christopher Chabris and Daniel Simons `www.theinvisiblegorilla.com`.

Intuition-based decision making is therefore prone to serious inaccuracies and errors. Yet, intuition and instinct are still the most commonly used basis for important and sometimes critical decisions by senior executives and managers. How does one gauge which items to place on the shelves of retail or grocery stores? What is the underlying commonality among customers or patrons? What are the main drivers of customers' behavioral and buying patterns?

The combination of intuition and domain knowledge has and will always be instrumental in driving businesses forward. Yet, data-backed decision making is much more powerful. Data hold the promise of providing accurate documen-

Figure 1.1: An example of an optical illusion: impossible objects.

tation of the past. Such objective documentation is necessary for improving awareness, enhancing understanding, and detecting unusual events in the past. Armed with a better understanding of the past, there is a better chance of improving decision making which affects the future.

Data are often viewed as the low level of abstraction from which *information* and then *knowledge* and *intelligence* can be derived. The term "data" means different things to different people. To computer scientists, "raw data" means bits and bytes or strings of zeros and ones. Journalists think of data as facts. In the business intelligence or analytics context, data mean a set of measurements on a set of records. For example, marketing data might include measurements on a million customers that include customer demographics, purchase history, etc. Financial data might include various financial performance indexes for a set of firms. And of course there are data that integrate information from multiple sources (financial, marketing, operations, etc.).

Sometimes a certain data source can provide different types of data. For example, a telecommunications company can extract data that contains calling and data usage information for a set of phone numbers. In this case, records are individual phone numbers and the measurements are usage-related metrics. Alternatively, we can extract aggregated revenue and usage data on a different set of records: the set of services or packages offered by the telecom (such as a prepaid calling package or an unlimited data program) or even on a set of different geographical regions. "Data" in the business analytics context always requires defining what is a record of interest and what are the available measurements.

Generating insights from data requires transforming the data in its raw form into information that is comprehensible to humans. Humans excel in detecting patterns in data when the data are provided in bite size (although they also find patterns in random data). For example, a domain expert may be able to uncover a trend or pattern in a spreadsheet that includes information on several hundreds of customers' credit card transactions with a dozen columns of measurements[2].

[2] Even with small samples, it is often difficult for humans to detect patterns and to distinguish real patterns from random ones.

However, the more typical scenario today is thousands to millions of customers (rows) and hundreds to thousands of measurements (columns). Human experts, no matter how much domain expertise and experience they possess, do not have the capacity to extract patterns or insights from such large amounts of data without the aid of analytics software and knowledge.

The overwhelming amounts of data that are now available to organizations and individuals are successfully described by Mitchell Kapor's saying[3]

> *Getting information off the Internet is like taking a drink from a fire hydrant.*

[3] Mitchell Kapor is founder of Lotus Development Corp. and the designer of the early spreadsheet software Lotus 1-2-3. He was the first chair of the Mozilla Foundation; www.kapor.com.

The growth of data beyond the limits of human perception has led to the development of technologies for deriving insight. Basic tools that aggregate or slice-and-dice data help in giving the user a better understanding of general trends and patterns. More sophisticated technology, such as the business analytics tools that we discuss in this book, helps users not only to understand the data, but to evaluate the potential of various actions and decisions. Our focus is on transforming data into actionable insights.

Given the huge amounts of data as well as human limitations, the real challenge is establishing a framework to sort through the deluge of data and transform the useful information into insights. One could dive even deeper by asking "Do you know what you do not know?" Is there any insight, knowledge or information that is currently hidden within the wealth of accumulated data that would improve business processes, uncover new growth potential, etc.? This is the birth of business analytics.

IPSA SCIENTIA POTESTAS EST (KNOWLEDGE IS POWER).

— Sir Francis Bacon (1561–1626)
Religious Meditations, of Heresies, 1597

1.2 *From Business Intelligence to Business Analytics*

Today's data-rich organizations seek methods for extracting value from their data. Management no longer asks *if* data hold value, but instead *how* value can be created from the company's data.

Fact-based decision making is not a new concept. But with the new volumes of data, there is a need for new methods and technologies to generate intelligence. Such methods should help *extract* and *analyze* large amounts of data from huge databases and data warehouses.

A decade ago, *business intelligence* was an umbrella term introduced to describe a variety of technologies that support data-based decision making. These include:

Data Management: consolidation, integration and management of data

Reporting: report generation that summarizes and conveys information from available data

Intelligence: automatic generation of insights from the available data.

Data management is a prerequisite for reporting and for more advanced intelligence extraction. Reporting is a basic approach for presenting data in aggregate, human-digestible form.

In earlier days, companies struggled to implement the first two components. "intelligence" within business intelligence did not get implemented from a systems point of view. Instead, it was supplemented by domain expertise (users' intelligence) through the interpretation of consolidated data reports (see Figure 1.2).

Even today, most companies struggle with non-trivial data management issues such as integrating data from different business units and disparate sources, extracting timely

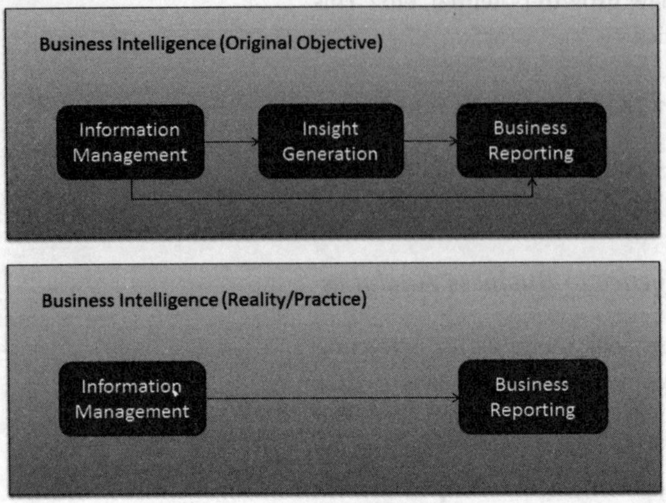

Figure 1.2: Illustration of business intelligence original objective as a focus area and the resulting actual implementations.

and useful samples from large databases, summarizing large amounts of data in aggregate form, and creating effective reports based on user-defined requirements.

Reports are currently still the most popular form of data analysis in the business world. Reports come in various formats such as PDF, HTML and most popularly — Microsoft Excel. Data aggregations are displayed in the form of tables and charts. Most organizations still rely on spreadsheet software for presenting reports to management. While spreadsheet tools can be powerful analytical tools, most organizations use only the most basic features. Most reporting tools are designed for database experts to use, often requiring knowledge of structured query language (SQL).

Business intelligence (BI) has thus become synonymous with data management and reporting. A main challenge with BI is that it does not form a closed loop where the generated insights lead to action, which in turn leads to changes in Key Performance Index (KPI). Two reasons for non-action are the lack of timeliness and the lack of an actionable process. Reports that take months to generate are often not useful by the time they reach the business stakeholder. In addition, often there is no corroboration as to who reads the reports, how often, what is gleaned from them, and what action is taken.

It is important to note that recent advances in data management and reporting tools have been empowering users to directly interact with large volumes of data. By "interact" we mean the ability to manipulate, query and explore data in a user-friendly way that does not require programming skills. This self-serve model does not require IT to be a proxy (and sometimes a bottleneck) for different business users to interact with data. While most organizations still use traditional tools made by the large software vendors, a growing number of companies are moving to self-serve software. One such advance is the recent field of *Visual Analytics* which provides users with effective ways to visualize their data.

In particular, state-of-the-art data visualization tools provide the capability to create, use, and share *interactive dashboards*. A dashboard is comprised of a set of linked charts and tables of data, which provide multiple views. Users can interact with the data via the dashboard by means of sliders, filters and other gadgets, similar to the interactive nature of applications such as Google Maps. An example of an interactive dashboard[4] is shown in Figure 1.3. Another recent trend is pushing reporting capabilities to portable devices for consumption on-the-go as shown in Figure 1.4. When built effectively, such dashboards support users in exploring trends, patterns and anomalies in the data. In addition, various self-serve reporting tools allow non-technical users to query data and generate ad hoc reports.

[4] The dashboard is available at `liberation.galitshmueli.com/data-liberation-through-visualization`.

Note that the term "analytics" is sometimes used to describe data reporting and other BI activities. For example, *Web Analytics* is "the measurement, collection, analysis and reporting of internet data for purposes of understanding and optimizing web usage."[5] Google Analytics, currently the most widely used Web Analytics service, is a powerful reporting and visualization tool of web usage statistics (see Figure 1.5)[6].

[5] Web Analytics article on Wikipedia, accessed Aug 15, 2012.

[6] Google Analytics' approach is to show high-level, dashboard-type data for the casual user, and more in-depth data further into the report set.

While data management and reporting tools have become more user-friendly and therefore offer better support to domain experts, they still heavily rely on the user to generate intelligence.

Business analytics, a relatively new term, was coined to address this gap in the business intelligence realm. Despite the recent buzz and focus on "the business analytics paradigm shift," there is ongoing confusion as to the fundamental difference between business intelligence and business analytics (see Box). It is not uncommon to see the two terms used interchangeably. In fact, many organizations believe that reporting historical trends is akin to business analytics.

While a variety of definitions exists for business analytics,

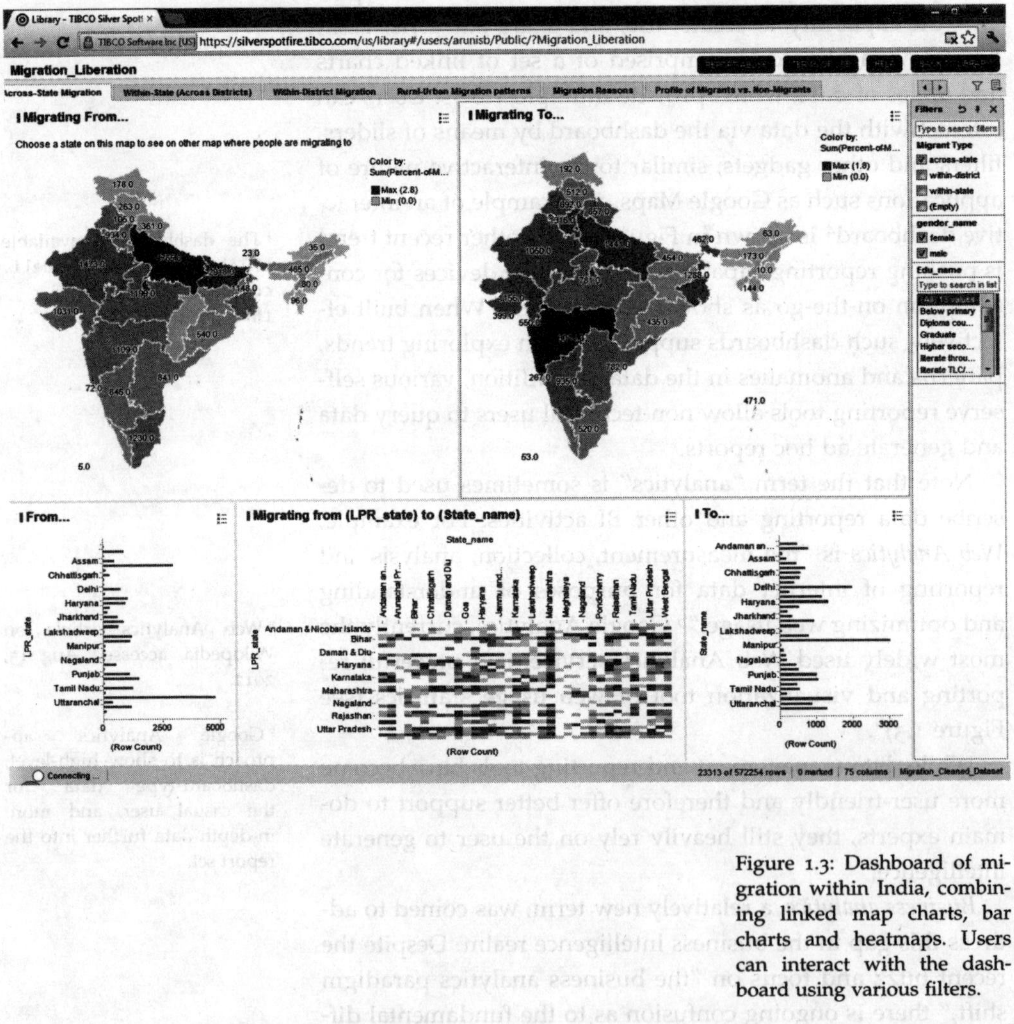

Figure 1.3: Dashboard of migration within India, combining linked map charts, bar charts and heatmaps. Users can interact with the dashboard using various filters.

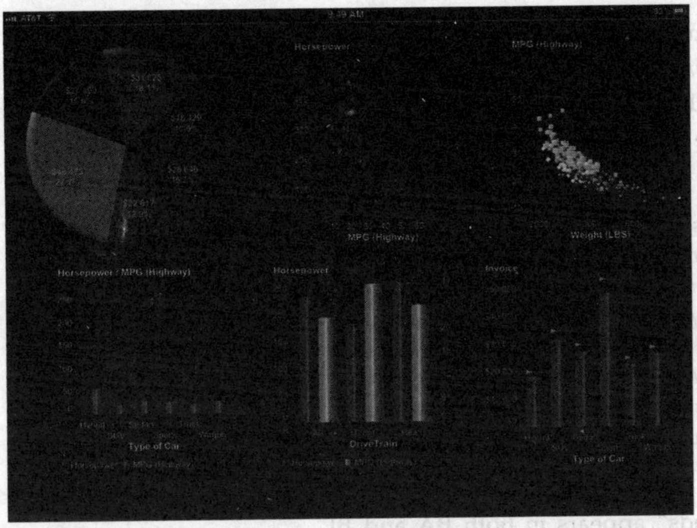

Figure 1.4: Dashboard of SAS Mobile BI Reporting on an iPad. Users can interact with the dashboard using various filters.

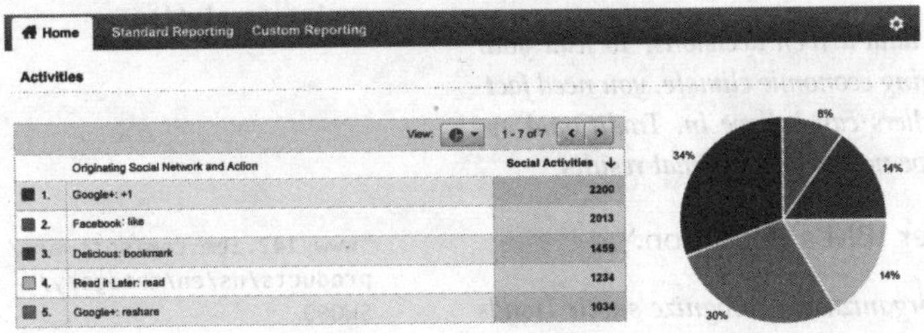

Figure 1.5: Example of Google Analytics dashboard (from www.google.com/analytics).

we focus on the key feature which distinguishes BA from BI: *system-generated intelligence* based on automated data analysis. This new layer includes a range of analytic techniques, from statistical methods to machine learning algorithms, that not only sift through large datasets but also generate automated actionable intelligence. These capabilities, beyond simple reporting and data exploration, are often termed *data mining*. An important aspect that distinguishes BA from BI is the integration of BA outputs and models as interventions into the business process, thereby forming a closed loop that allows measurement of business benefits.

Confusion exists regarding the term *business analytics* and how it differs from *business intelligence*. We quote several popular current definitions to illustrate the confusion.

On Wikipedia, the article on *Business analytics* opens with the following description:[7]

> *Business analytics (BA) refers to the skills, technologies, applications and practices for continuous iterative exploration and investigation of past business performance to gain insight and drive business planning. Business analytics focuses on developing new insights and understanding of business performance based on data and statistical methods. In contrast, business intelligence traditionally focuses on using a consistent set of metrics to both measure past performance and guide business planning, which is also based on data and statistical methods.*

[7] en.wikipedia.org/wiki/Business_analytics accessed August 1, 2012.

Note that "statistical methods" appears in both BA and BI definitions.

Software company SAS[8] defines business analytics as:

> *Enabling faster, more accurate data-driven decisions: To lead your organization in today's challenging economic climate, you need fact-based answers that you and others can believe in. Traditional approaches to decision support have not yielded optimal results.*

[8] www.sas.com/businessanalytics.

Service and software provider IBM's definition:[9]

> *Business analytics helps your organization recognize subtle trends and patterns so you can anticipate and shape events and improve outcomes. Not only can you drive more top-line growth and control costs, you can also identify risks that could derail your plans - and take timely corrective action.*

[9] www-142.ibm.com/software/products/us/en/category/SWQ00.

Consulting firm Accenture mentions business analytics: [10]

> *High performance hinges on the ability to gain insights from data-insights that inform better decisions and strengthen customer relationships.*

[10] www.accenture.com/us-en/consulting/analytics/Pages/index.aspx.

These definitions and descriptions capture the ambiguity surrounding the terms business analytics and business intelligence.

Both the field of data analytics and its associated terminology are in flux; for a summary of terms that is updated on a regular basis, see `www.statistics.com/data-analytics`.

1.3 *Levels of "Intelligence"*

Before discussing how business analytics can aid organizations to improve their decision making process, we first revisit the terminology and the analytics components that separate BI from BA. The degree of intelligence, i.e., sophistication of the analytic technology and its potential value to an organization can be illustrated as a two dimensional graph of analytical maturity, measured by intelligence vs. business value.

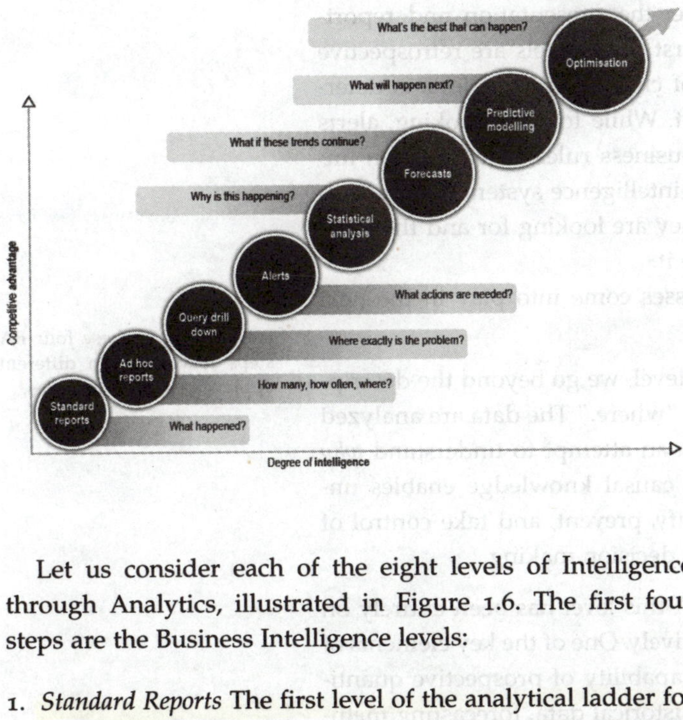

Figure 1.6: Intelligence Through Analytics: The eight levels of analytics from Business Intelligence to business analytics. Note that this is a general representation and that the order of analytical steps may vary in different applications and for different industries.

Let us consider each of the eight levels of Intelligence through Analytics, illustrated in Figure 1.6. The first four steps are the Business Intelligence levels:

1. *Standard Reports* The first level of the analytical ladder focuses on understanding what has happened. For example, reviewing a company's annual report and pinpointing various events. Sample questions that a report can answer include: "What was sold? What was purchased? What was the volume of fraudulent cases detected?"

2. *Ad Hoc Reports* After gaining knowledge of events through the standard reports, secondary questions may surface such as "When did it happen? How many times did it occur during a particular period of time?" Reports are then generated to answer the particular questions of interest.

3. *Query Drilldowns – Online Analytical Processing (OLAP)* Diving deeper into the event, answering questions such as "Where did the event happen? Where exactly was the problem?"

4. *Alerts* The concluding stage of the first four levels is the generation of alerts. Based on critical events learned from the previous three levels, we are able to act upon and react to future critical events by triggering business-specific alerts. In addition, guidelines are created for post-alert actions.

These four levels are the foundation of standard business operations in almost all organizations. The four levels are part of business intelligence: the presentation and reporting of historical data. The first three levels are retrospective in nature. The fourth step of creating future alerts is determined by the domain expert. While forward looking, alerts are based on user-defined business rules. Therefore, an important aspect of a business intelligence system is users' advance knowledge of what they are looking for and the basic analysis required to produce it.

Business analytical processes come into play in the next four levels[11]:

[11] The order of these four BA steps may differ in different applications and industries.

5. *Statistical Analysis* In this level, we go beyond the descriptive realms of "what" and "where." The data are analyzed using statistical models in an attempt to understand *why* the event occurred. Such causal knowledge enables understanding how to identify, prevent, and take control of events, which then guides decision making.

6. *Forecasting* The focus until this level has been entirely on deriving insight retrospectively. One of the key elements of business analytics is the capability of prospective quantitative forecasting. Using historical data, forecasting methods identify past patterns and trends in the data and use those to create future forecasts of overall behavior. This level helps answer questions such as "What will quarterly sales look like next year?"

7. *Predictive Modeling* Taking the forecasting concept one step further and expanding beyond time-related forecasts, predictive modeling generates future predictions for individual records. Unlike forecasting, prediction deals with individual events rather than overall trends. Another distinction between forecasting and predictive modeling is that

forecasting looks at measurements over time and generates future forecasts. Predictive modeling looks at measurements of many records at a single point in time, and uses those to generate predictions for new records.

8. *Optimization* Optimization methods combine the generated intelligence to optimize business processes or objectives, given operational and other constraints. This level, utilizing causal insights, forecasts and/or predictions from previous levels, answers questions such as "How to maximize profit subject to infrastructure constraints? How to optimally allocate resources subject to a set of priorities?"

These last four levels comprise the core of business analytics. They aim to uncover insights from historical data and generate projections into the future, using analytical processes in alignment with business requirements.

The ability to identify indicators of an outcome of interest is key to business analytics. The London Fire Brigade (LFB)[12] used business analytics to identify which homes (who?), among the millions of homes in London, were most at risk for a fire, as well as the key indicators of high fire risk (what?). With such information, LFB is better equipped to prevent future fires and save lives. The data were integrated from multiple sources, including census data and population demographics, land type, lifestyle data, historic incidents and past prevention activity. Analysts then used predictive modelling to predict which homes were most at risk. They used statistical analysis to identify those indicators most predictive of fire risk.

[12] Copyright ©SAS Institute Inc. Cary, NC, USA `www.sas.com/success/LondonFireBrigade.html`.

It is important to understand that analyzing the relationship between indicators and an outcome requires collecting data that are available *prior* to the event, in addition to data summarizing the outcome (how many fires?). For example, identifying key indicators to predict job-related accidents requires not only information on accident type and outcome but also data on the circumstances of the event and information on employers, nature of job, weather conditions, employee health information, etc.[13]. As predictions of future events will be based on such indicators, it is important that the indicator information be available at the time of prediction.

[13] *New York Times*, How Companies Learn Your Secrets `www.nytimes.com/2012/02/19/magazine/shopping-habits.html`.

Let us illustrate the full eight-level picture by examining a case of customer complaints at a call center. Examples of questions and insights generated at each of the levels could be as follows:

Standard Report How many complaints have been recorded, by product and/or channel (phone call, email, Facebook page, etc.)?

Ad Hoc Report Compare complaint volume of a specific brand with another brand.

Query Drill-down Which channel is causing the greatest problem?

Alerts Set an alert when a KPI exceeds/nears a given threshold for investigation/action.

Statistical Analysis What are the most significant factors associated with complaints?

Forecasting What will be the number of complaints in the next quarter?

Predictive Modeling Which complaints from which customer segments are most likely to escalate?

Optimization What is the best deployment of available resources for maximizing complaint resolution?

The last four levels are the business analytics components. These are forward-looking, rely heavily on data availability and on data analytics tools to generate intelligence.

MOST PEOPLE USE STATISTICS THE WAY A DRUNKARD USES A LAMP POST, MORE FOR SUPPORT THAN ILLUMINATION.

— Samuel Langhorne Clemens (Mark Twain) (1835–1910)
American Author and Humorist

2 *The Business Analytics Cycle*

A business analytics implementation consists of four main components: a business problem and context, data, data-analytic tools, and solution implementation within the business context. These components are tightly coupled within the life cycle of a business analytics project. Figure 2.1 gives a schematic view of the process that an organization would follow in a BA project. Note the close integration of the business and analytics contexts. Figure 2.1 illustrates the following process:

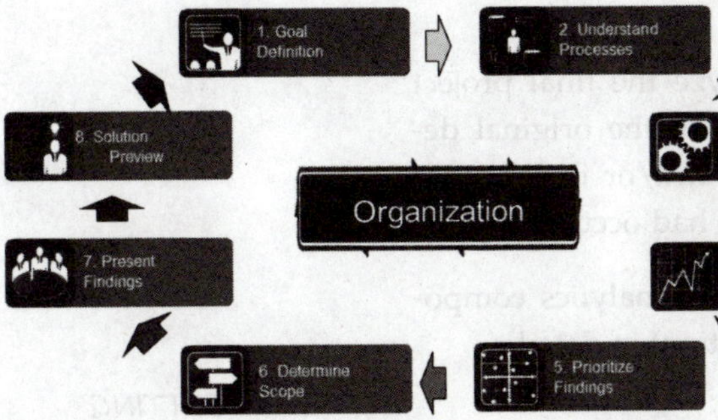

Figure 2.1: Illustration of a suggested organizational discovery process for business analytics projects.

1. **Define the Objective** (1) What is the business objective? Examples include process improvement, cost reduction, and operational efficiency. (2) What is the analytic objective? For instance, predict churn, detect fraud, create product segments, generate recommendations, or forecast demand.

2. **Understand the Process** What are the business processes associated with the identified business objective?

3. **Specify Integration Requirements** What are the required data sources? What is their availability? Can they be inte-

grated? Technological effort is required in this step.

4. **Identify Areas for Solution** List all identified areas for business analytics solutions for discussion and verification. Has anything in the previous three steps been missed?

5. **Prioritize Findings** Usually, multiple potential projects will be identified. It is important to prioritize the list based on benefit to the organization and the expected complexity.

6. **Determine Scope** Determine a realistic analytical scope for selected project(s). Predetermine projects' expected ROI, outcomes and criteria of success. The BA solution implementation begins after this step.

7. **Present Findings** Review the analytical outcome regularly with stakeholders for solution process and progress. Interim insights can lead to modification of the original objective. It is crucial to gain the support of stakeholders throughout the project as well as ensure continuous verification by domain experts.

8. **Solution Preview** Review and analyze the final project benefits and insights. Verify these with the original defined objectives. If different benefits and/or insights are generated, analyze *why* the difference had occurred.

Let us examine each of the four business analytics components (objective, data, tools, implementation) in detail.

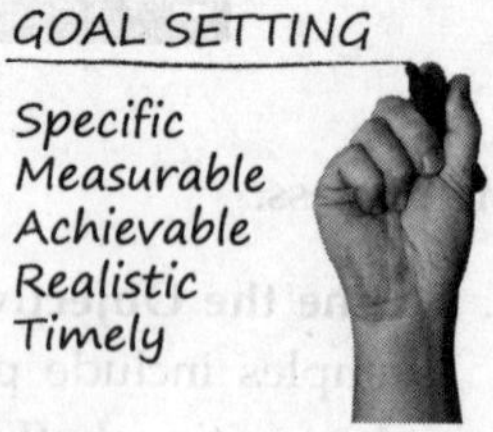

2.1 *Objective*

Business problems are typically not framed as well defined business analytics problems. Adopting a business analytics approach begins with identifying a business challenge or a potential benefit of interest. Once the business opportunity is identified, it must be converted into a business analytics problem. The conversion requires collaboration and clear communication between the stakeholders that will be affected by the solution and the analysts implementing the project.

A business analytics problem requires defining the business problem in terms of specific measurements, specific outcome metrics, and specific performance requirements. This process requires an understanding of the specific business pain points, the KPIs[1] in question and the amount of improvement that we expect to see in these KPIs. For example, a business objective of reducing customer churn could be converted into the BA objective of identifying, within a large customer base, those customers who are most likely to churn. "Churn" must be defined clearly, as in customers who do not return within three months. If success is measured in terms of costs, then information on the cost of churn and customer acquisition, if not readily available, should be gathered. The time frame of the project and its deployment are other objective-related details that need to be decided.

[1] Key Performance Index.

Once the BA objective is set, an internal assessment of readiness setup and required skill-set is conducted jointly with representatives from the organization's IT department along with other business units and management. It is critical that management assume full responsibility for a business analytics initiative in collaboration with the relevant business units. The cooperation of the latter is crucial, because the operations and outcomes of such an initiative will have a direct impact on their operations.

The internal assessment may be complemented with a discovery process that allows an organization to identify and prioritize its findings with regard to the key challenges of identifying the right questions and relevant data. As a best practice, it is advised to align the discovery and business questions with the eight steps described in the previous section. It is important that all stakeholders clearly understand what can readily and realistically be achieved.

2.2 *Data*

In order to implement BA, a necessary component is data. Data must be available, accurate, timely, rich, and in sufficient amounts. Data can include numerical measurements, geographical information, textual and any other form of information deemed relevant to the objective. Recall that "data" in the business analytics context refers to a set of measurements on a set of records. It is important to have a clear definition of what the record of interest is (for example, a customer, a transaction, a product, a user account, an email address). It is also important that the analysts understand the meaning of the different measurements, where they came from, and their availability at the time of deployment.

Misunderstandings can lead to results that are useless at best and disastrous at worst. Numerous disasters have resulted from misunderstanding the measuring unit. In 1999, NASA lost a Mars orbiter due to confusing metric and English units[2]. A similar confusion caused an Air Canada plane to run out of fuel in the midst of a flight[3].

[2] www.riverdeep.net/current/1999/10/100199.mars_explorer.jhtml.

[3] hawaii.hawaii.edu/math/Courses/Math100/Chapter1/Extra/CanFlt143.htm.

Assuring the availability of measurements at the time of deployment is also critical. For example, consider a model for forecasting daily air quality based on same-day weather reports. While we might have a dataset that contains both daily air quality measurements and weather reports for a certain year, it is impossible to deploy the model in practice because weather reports are unavailable prior to the date of interest. Replacing weather reports with weather forecasts can lead to a completely different model.

Data integrated across business units from disparate data sources offer higher chances of useful discovery and meeting the BA objective. Data quality and quantity vary drastically between industries and even between different units of a single organization. Whether the data contain sufficient information for meeting the business analytics objective is often unknown at the start of the journey. Yet even failure to achieve the goal can lead to a better understanding of which types of data need to be collected, to changes in ways data are captured or stored, and other data-related insights that will enable the next business analytics implementation. Hence an important step in any business analytics analysis is data exploration for the purpose of understanding the quality and relevancy of the data to the underlying objective. Similarly, such an exploration may aid in the identification of data issues that are easy to detect (see an illustration of data visualization in Figure 2.2).

Organizations have varied entry points for their business analytics, as well as business intelligence, journey. Some organizations commence from user requirements (top-down), while others commence from data availability (bottom-up). The best practice for business analytics solution design and implementation is to start with defining an objective but to closely combine user requirements with data availability. Such integration promotes the drive for new insight while assuring realistic assumptions about data availability (see Figure 2.3).

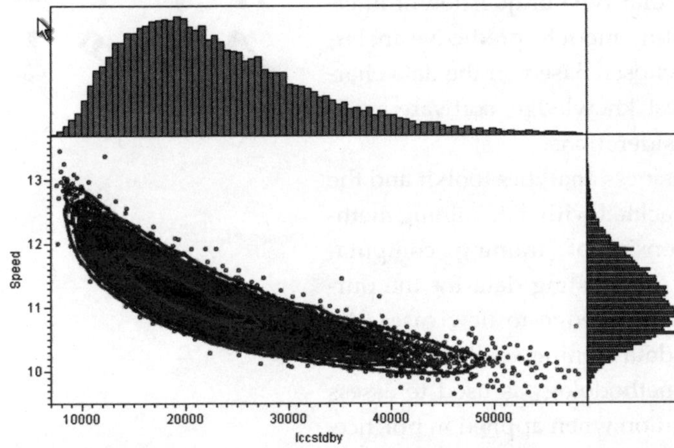

Figure 2.2: Example of data visualization; A scatter plot with non-parametric density contours and marginal distributions.

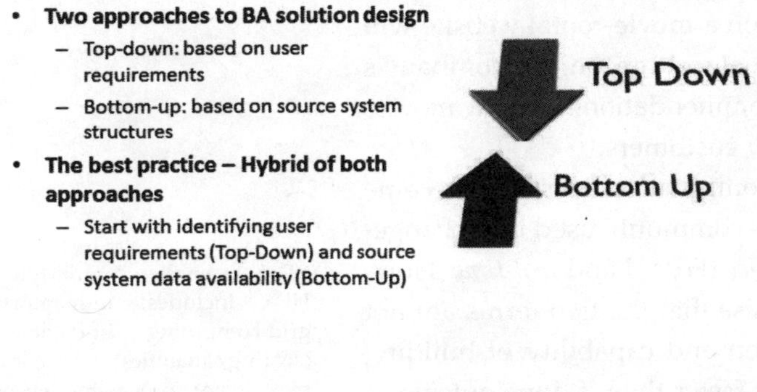

Figure 2.3: Approaches toward identification and implementation of business analytics solutions.

2.3 *Analytic Tools and Methods*

Given an objective and data, a set of BA tools and technologies are applied to the data to achieve the goal of interest. Returning to the four types of BA tools (Figure 1.6), methods are chosen based on the particular type of question of interest. Statistical analysis, forecasting models, predictive analytics and optimization tools are chosen based on the data characteristics, the objective, analyst knowledge, software availability and computational considerations.

Chapter 3 introduces the business analytics toolkit and the types of questions that can be tackled with data mining methods. The process of analysis consists of "training" computational methods to learn from our existing data for the purpose of applying the learned knowledge to new cases. An important component of the data mining toolkit is performance evaluation. A careful methodology is used to assess the performance of the BA solution when applied in practice, and to compare it to other realistic benchmarks. We elaborate on these points in Chapter 3.

2.4 *Implementation*

When the data mining solution has been deemed satisfactory, it is then deployed. Deployment means that the model that was trained on the historical data will now be used to generate predictions, forecasts or other values of interest for new cases. This process is called "scoring new data."

For example, a data mining algorithm developed to provide movie recommendations on a movie-rental website will be deployed by launching the algorithm on the company's website, thereby providing recommendations for new movies ("scoring") to existing and new customers.

During implementation, computational issues become critical. In particular, two terms commonly used interchangeably are *high-performance analytics* (HPA)[4] and *real-time*. However, it is important to emphasise that the two terms are not identical. HPA is the facilitation and capability of building (developing) analytical models faster than if done outside of a HPA environment.

[4] The technology underlying HPA includes; in-memory, grid-computing, in-database (scoring/analytics), complex event processing/event streaming, real-time scoring.

HPA relates specifically to speeding up the modeling stage. Furthermore, HPA is commonly associated with the term "Big Data" when the volume, velocity and variety of data exceeds an organization's storage or computing capacity for accurate and timely decision-making.

> BIG DATA IS A SHORTHAND LABEL THAT TYPICALLY MEANS APPLYING THE TOOLS OF ARTIFICIAL INTELLIGENCE, LIKE MACHINE LEARNING, TO VAST NEW TROVES OF DATA BEYOND THAT CAPTURED IN STANDARD DATABASES. THE NEW DATA SOURCES INCLUDE WEB-BROWSING DATA TRAILS, SOCIAL NETWORK COMMUNICATIONS, SENSOR DATA AND SURVEILLANCE DATA.
>
> — *New York Times* reporter Steve Lohr
> "How Big Data Became So Big", August 12, 2012

Consider the example of Catalina Marketing[5], a company that helps retailers identify what coupons, advertisements and information messages to present to customers at checkout. Catalina realized that the current process of capturing shoppers' behavior lagged behind the changes in shopping patterns.

[5] Copyright ©SAS Institute Inc. Cary, NC, USA www.sas.com/success/catalina.html

Incorporating HPA allowed the time needed to model and analyze data related to around 250 million transactions processed per week to be reduced from over a month to just days, which under the current definitions would not be construed as real-time. However, the underlying business benefit meant that Catalina was better equipped to model changes in customers' behavior in an on-going manner. This enabled Catalina to extend more relevant offers to customers at point of checkout.

So what is real-time? "Real-time" is the ability to score data in a near-instantaneous manner. Reverting back to the Catalina example, it took several days to build the customer behavior models (not real time) which were then used to score (real-time) customers at checkout.

The requirement for real-time scoring may not entail a requirement for fast model development (HPA). In the Catalina case both were needed. Most organizations require real-time scoring capabilities, as they allow the surfacing of knowledge relevant for decision making processes. For example, consider the following question: is this credit card transaction or broker trade fraudulent? Rather than having a quarterly, or even weekly financial risk assessment, it is critical to identify the risk for loans, products, customers, etc. at the point of transaction.

INSANITY: DOING THE SAME THING OVER AND OVER AGAIN AND EXPECTING DIFFERENT RESULTS.

— Albert Einstein (1879-1955)
Theoretical Physicist

2.5 *Guiding Questions*

Below are questions to help guide the business analytics process. Our list is far from extensive, but gives the flavor of the types of questions that the analyst should construct. Considering such questions can help reduce the uncertainty regarding different aspects, components, and requirements that will appear as the business analytics project unfolds.

Business Objectives

1. What are some of the challenges with the current state processes that are impeding progress?

2. What are the specific high level key performance objectives?

3. How do we envision business analytics assisting in achieving our vision?

Data

1. What are the various source systems applicable to this project (Examples include Siebel, SAP, Oracle ERP, flat files and Microsoft Excel)?

2. What is the number of data tables in the source systems? What is the size of the database?

3. What are the current methods for data extraction, transformation and loading (ETL)?

4. Are the data structured, unstructured, or a combination?

5. How quickly can data be obtained from different sources?

6. Can data from different sources be easily merged?

7. How much history is available for each data source?

Analytical Tools and Methods

Business Intelligence

1. Which data sources are currently used for creating dashboards and reports?

2. What BI capabilities are currently being used?

3. What questions are currently being answered using BI?

4. What BI software is available?

Forecasting

1. Does forecasting rely mainly on spreadsheet calculations?

2. Are there any current unresolved forecasting issues?

3. Is there an operational planning process that the forecasts serve? (for example, an HR or financial planning process)

Predictive Modeling

1. How can predictive modeling be applied to our daily work?

2. Are we currently applying any segmentation or clustering? If so, to what end?

3. Where and how do we collect analytical data? Do we request data extracts from IT, or do users perform this task themselves?

Implementation

1. Do we need real-time (or near-real-time) solutions or can we wait longer for results?

2. Is the analytics solution a one time endeavor or a recurring application?

3. What is the analytical expertise of the end user? How automated should the solution be?

4. What resources will be available for implementation in the future?

2.6 *Requirements for Integrating Business Analytics*

There is now compelling evidence that adopting business analytics as a paradigm is crucial for growth and effectiveness. Research conducted by *Bloomberg Businessweek* suggests that "The more an organization relies on analytics in the decision-making process, the more effective it will be"[6].

[6] www.scribd.com/doc/85156721/Current-State-of-Business-Analytics.

The growing adoption of business analytics by governments and businesses puts those who do not use analytics at a disadvantage. Adopting a BA approach means a change in the entire organization's mindset: the organization prioritizes data-based decision making, puts processes in place and invests in resources so that a data-oriented approach can thrive and add value. BA is not just an adoption of a new technology. It is much more than just purchasing software and hiring a group of technically-savvy engineers.

Vision and Managerial Leadership

Like any paradigm shift, management and senior support for business analytics is fundamental to change and success. For an organization-wide business analytics adoption to achieve the maximum business outcome, it is imperative to develop sound strategy that meets short-term needs and provides the foundation for the organization's long-term vision.

Because the BA paradigm requires a change in mindset, its success is dependent on leadership, not only acceptance, by management. Implementing a business analytics project is only half the story, as outcomes and insights need to be acted on to achieve their potential benefits. Acting on such insights can result in changes to organizational processes and key performance indicators (KPI). For example, a supply chain optimization solution might imply that the current business objective KPIs lead to sub-optimal solutions, and therefore require re-evaluation or modification of current supply chain practices.

A real-world example is the operational challenge that banks face in replenishing their ATM network. While most banks commonly outsource their operation execution to third-party vendors, the implications of replenishment policies directly affect the bank.

The public holds the bank accountable for ATMs that have run out of cash ("cash-out"). An optimal replenishment schedule is typically based on an inventory optimization procedure that considers supply and demand: minimizing costs of replenishment trips and minimizing cash-out events while maximizing cash utilization. However, and more importantly, the implementation of such a solution raises operational constraints that may not have initially been spelled out (for example, that replenishment trips can only take place during certain hours). Hence, the insights that the BA approach generates help establish a framework for banks to simulate KPI assumptions and objectives, even before these are set.

The application of business analytics may be driven by individual, departmental or enterprise-wide requirements. In all cases, the various stakeholders must recognize and accept the BA approach. A cross-organization spirit of cooperation is necessary because BA relies on defining business objectives that often affect more than individual departments, and because it is useful to use data from across the organization.

Analytics Skills

The increase in adoption of business analytics is mirrored by the increase in demand for analytical talent, where the current demand far exceeds the supply. The Bloomberg Businessweek Research Service report[7] states that "Nearly half of survey respondents say their organisations place a premium on workers with analytical skills ... Inability to use analytics to make decisions and lack of appropriate analytical talent are two of the main issues inhibiting companies in their Business Analytics initiatives."

[7] Copyright ©SAS Institute Inc. Cary, NC, USA `www.sas.com/offices/europe/uk/press_office/press_releases/Aug/Business_analytics.html`.

The first concern in adopting BA is the required skill sets. *What are the job requirements for business analytics experts?* Because BA requires a tight connection between the business context and the analytics implementation, it is insufficient to have only technical skills or business expertise. Business Analytics champions are those who understand the business environment and the fundamentals of business analytics. They can point out opportunities where business analytics can lead to potential improvements, and can lead and monitor the analytics journey within the organization. An in-house analytics team usually consists of one or more BA champions and a set of technical analysts (statisticians, data miners, etc.). The team proposes and implements BA solutions in close communication with the stakeholders in the organization.

The level of technical expertise needed depends on the application and industry. Despite common perceptions, BA software tools do not always require statisticians or PhDs, although they *do* require individuals who are analytically inclined. Organizations that have BA champions but lack sufficient technical expertise for implementing the BA solution might use an external analytics firm for that purpose.

However, it is imperative for in-house BA champions to lead the effort and to be completely involved in the analysts' work. A recent development in this arena is crowdsourcing companies, such as CrowdANALYTIX[8] or data mining competitions such as those on Kaggle.com, where the technical component is outsourced to a large audience of analysts. The challenge is to accurately convert the business challenge into a well-defined business analytics problem.

[8] CrowdANALYTIX is a global community of experts on BA, competing and collaborating on BA projects, with the objective of optimizing business outcomes www.crowdanalytix.com.

Another risk is that at time of implementation, the technical solution might not perform appropriately. An example illustrating this risk is the Netflix Prize contest[9].

[9] www.netflixprize.com.

The online movie-rental company Netflix wanted to improve the performance of its movie recommendation engine. In 2007, after defining a specific BA task and performance metrics, the company released a large dataset of millions of records to the public. The challenge was to improve the Netflix recommendation engine performance by more than 10%. The first prize was set at one million US dollars. The goal was reached at the conclusion of the two-year contest by a team of data miners and statisticians, and the prize was awarded in exchange for the winning algorithm.

However, the new recommendation system never was implemented. By the competition's end, Netflix had already moved from their earlier DVD-by-mail model to mainly a streaming model. The technical solution was no longer applicable[10].(Data about actual movie-watching behavior in the streaming model can lead to better recommendations altogether).

[10] techblog.netflix.com/2012/04/netflix-recommendations-\penalty-\@Mbeyond-5-stars.html.

An example of how in-house implementations can avoid such discrepancies is a customer churn project by the HP Global Analytics group, which provides internal BA capabilities within Hewlett Packard. The analytics group developed a model for predicting repeat purchase of HP products. While the original model developed by the team performed well in terms of predictive power, it was not practical to implement because it could not generate predictions sufficiently fast on the huge customer datasets. The analytics team then came up with an approximate data mining algorithm that "can score massive databases for repeat purchase in real time"[11].

[11] "Customer Targeting Framework: Scalable Repeat Purchase Scoring Algorithm for Large Databases" (2012), Pal, Sinha, Saha, Jaumann, and Misra, *IPCSIT* vol. 25 (2012) www.ipcsit.com/vol25/028-ICMLC2012-L1012.pdf.

Software

In terms of software, a common question is which software package to use for business analytics. The variety of software is large and growing, from open-source to commercial, from software that requires programming knowledge to drag-and-click and menu-driven software, from cloud-based solutions to hard-drive centric, from freeware to expensive but vendor-supported paid licensing, from industry-specific software to generic tools.

Reviews and comparisons of different products are available through various reports and surveys such as the annual Rexer Analytics Survey[12] or the KDnuggets Data Mining Community website[13].

[12] www.rexeranalytics.com/Data-Miner-Survey-2011-\penalty-\@MIntro2.html.

[13] www.kdnuggets.com/software/suites.html.

Software vendors use varying definitions of "business intelligence" and "business analytics" and it is often unclear what a particular product is actually capable of. To assist in software choice, we describe the questions one should ask to determine whether a particular solution is indeed BA-capable.

The anchor that differentiates a BI solution from a BA solution, is BA's ability to accommodate most of, if not all, levels 5–8 in Figure 1.6. Some software products have excellent data drilling and reporting tools. They may even have strong data visualization capabilities, but they lack more advanced data mining tools.

The term "data mining" is sometimes used to denote data management. To avoid confusion, it is advisable to request the list of data mining algorithms and statistical models that are supported by the software. After reading this book, it should be clear whether the list includes only data management and reporting tools as opposed to automated data mining techniques.

Lastly, we note that the boundaries between the eight levels in terms of software are thinning, given recent technological advances. In particular, some BI tools are now able to "embed" external BA tools. This occurs, for instance, when a BI vendor acquires a BA tool and integrates the two via embedding.

One example is TIBCO's BI tool Spotfire[14] that allows calling routines from the open-source statistical programming language S+/R. Another is SAP's BusinessObjects, which

[14] www.spotfire.tibco.com.

supports using IBM's SPSS Modeller software as a back-end statistical engine. There are many more examples, and the landscape is dynamic thanks to the changing OEM agreements and company purchases.

Learning from Failures

The buzz surrounding BA has focused on success stories of organizations that successfully reduced risk, increased their revenue, realized greater profits, and detected fraudulent transactions. Realistically, many projects fail to achieve their goal. However, failures are an important component of the BA process, as they allow the organization and the BA team to learn. The lessons are sometimes as important as the initial goals.

There are many unknowns that arise in the BA process, especially at the beginning of the journey. It is important to recognize the value of learning from failure and to legitimize failure as part of the BA process. The possibility of failure and potential reasons for failure should be discussed at an early assessment stage, and continuously raised during the project lifetime. Alertness to challenges can lead to timely modifications of the different components: the project objective, the data used in the project, the choice and use of analytical methods, and implementation.

Failure in itself is an important data collection issue. In many BA projects, the goal is to distinguish between successful and failed events. For example, in customer churn applications we want to identify repeat customers, whereas in fraud detection we want to discriminate fraudulent from non-fraudulent transactions. In such applications it is critical to collect data not only on the successes (returning customers, non-fraudulent transactions), but also on the failures. In the absence of failures, data mining methods will be unable to learn the difference between success and failure. Capital One Financial Corp., for instance, knowingly gives high-risk customers random amounts of credit in order to learn how they behave. This is the only way to gather information about the more-prone-to-failure population segment.

While roadblocks and challenges are to be expected in the analytical journey, the success of a BA application is fundamentally constrained by several factors — resistance to change, lack of technology and skills, and imagination. As we emphasized earlier, the mandate to pursue a business analytics approach in an organization must come from management and spread throughout the organization. Ultimately, the success of any BA program lies in the ability of the leaders to understand the potential of BA and to envision the possibilities at the time of ideation. Resistance to change is always a stumbling block, and a good way to diffuse it is by starting with a small-scale non-threatening BA project that showcases the usefulness of the new approach.

Investment in human and computing resources is essential. Hiring the right team and providing adequate training is paramount to the success of the organization's BA functionality. An adequate choice of technology is needed to enable the analytical journey.

Finally, imagination and mind-set are irrefutably the most challenging constraints to address. The true potential of BA can be elegantly summarized with the one line elevator pitch,

Do you know what you do not know?

2.7 *Common Questions*

The abundance of capabilities and techniques can easily complicate the question of what approach to use with a particular business problem. Although it is impossible to give an exact list of tools to match a certain business problem (due to the unique nature of each problem), there are a few common practices used to address these types of questions:[15]

[15] For details of data mining and data analytics techniques see Chapters 3 and 4.

- "I want to offer my customers recommendations for other products/services based on similar customers' actions."
  - One possibility is using Market Basket Analysis; a modeling technique that aims to identify what you are more or less likely to buy, given a group of items already acquired.
  - An alternative approach is to use Segmentation; a technique focused on identifying similar groups (clusters) of customers based on behavior (shopping) patterns (their attributes). Once these clusters have been created, it is then possible to identify and match a customer of interest with similar customers who have purchased products/services that our customer of interest has not purchased. Because this method is based on identifying behavioral similarity, it is reasonable to assume a high

chance of the customer being interested in these offerings.

- Finally, it is possible to build a product-specific predictive model, using a technique such as regression, based on historical customers who have purchased/not purchased the product to identify new customers most likely to purchase.

- "How do I get an idea of my customers' sentiments without using surveys?"

  - Do we have alternative data? These could exist in the form of emails, transcribed calls, etc. Alternatively, if these data sources are not available, are we able to identify and monitor customers' online identity (Facebook or Twitter page)? If so, we can then apply Text Analytics, and in particular Sentiment Analysis, to the crawled data sources (online or offline) to automatically identify and monitor the customer sentiment on a range of issues. Banks and telecommunication companies actively pursue these types of indirect assessment of customer sentiments toward products and services, as well as brand awareness.

- "How can I use my current customer database to reach out to similar customers?"

  - Segmentation (Clustering) of customer data allows identifying groups of customers with similar behavior. A bank can cluster its entire customer database, combining information from loans, accounts, and credit cards to identify clusters of similar customers. Such clustering and identification of similar behavior can be done even with limited information on potential customers. Online companies monitor clickstream and online behavior to identify similar customers — this gives rise to targeted online advertising.

- "I want to use my historical inventory data to better stock up in the future."

  - Forecasting and Optimization are two parts of such an operational process. First, we use historical data on inventory holdings (and utilization of SKU's[16]) to forecast expected supply and demand. Second, we deploy an

[16] Stock Keeping Units.

optimization engine which takes into account the underlying objective (minimum holding cost, maximum service level, etc.) together with operational constraints (limited shelf life of perishables, maximum holding per SKU, etc.). The forecasted information is fed into the optimization model to determine the best-possible inventory scenario.

- Software limitations: "My software does not have k-Nearest Neighbors (k-NN), should I buy a license for a new software package?"
  - It is likely that problems that require k-NN can be tackled using alternative modeling techniques (Naive Bayes, Classification Trees, etc.). However, if the particular k-NN algorithm is indeed required, most commercial (and professional) BA software allows for "add-ons" which expand capabilities. In general, it is not advisable to purchase an entire new suite for a single methodology unless it is core to the business.
- Production issues: "Our analytics team came up with two demand forecasting solutions. Which one should we choose? Will the solutions work when deployed to thousands of products?"
  - Consideration should be given in advance to how an analytical system will be operationalized, and whether there are any limitations (analytical or operational) that need to be considered.
  - A solution should not only be chosen based on good performance (such as high predictive power), but also on how it fits into the production stage. For that reason, solutions from crowd-sourcing and data mining competition websites are not always suitable to implement. See comment #2 on Kaggle forums `www.kaggle.com/forums/t/2065/when-is-it-better-to-keep-the-algorithm-to-yourself/11822`

Perspectives from a Practitioner

The following is a perspective from an industry practitioner. It is organized in FAQ format, reflecting common questions that are encountered in practice.

What is the purpose and goal of business analytics? To improve business performance. To help business be more effective. The ERP era saw a slew of transactional systems being implemented to automate every conceivable business process — planning, procurement, material receipt, manufacturing, asset management, finance and accounting, e-commerce, etc. These systems focused on efficiency. They focused on improving the number of transactions processed per unit of time. They focused on lowering the cost of processing transactions.

Due to the data being generated from these systems, it is now possible to identify the few customers, orders, invoices, programs that make the most impact, or, cause the most problems. Business analytics enables focused attention on the few things that matter most for the corporation, and hence improve effectiveness (as opposed to efficiency). An efficient call center will call a certain number of customers per day. An effective call center will call a different number of customers, possibly far fewer, but generate greater output (leads, comments, etc.)

With whom in the organization should we have a business analytics converzation? Always with leadership who have ownership of delivering business outcomes. Better marketing; better targeting; better lead generation; better collections management; better quality management; better Customer Satisfaction. These are typically LOB[17] leaders or functional leaders — Chief Marketing officer, Chief Risk officer, Chief Merchandising officer. Such stakeholders are typically measured and compensated by business metrics — revenue per employee, leads per $, marketing spend-to-sales, etc. Ironically, these metrics are often simple to define and explain, and are market oriented.

[17] Line of Business.

Stakeholders whose sole role is to achieve incremental control of costs are often less suitable business analytics partners.

What questions should we ask in our first conversation on business analytics? Key questions include:

- What business outcomes are you chartered to deliver?
- What are your business pains?
- What business challenge do you purport to solve?
- What specific business KPIs and measures are you considering to improve?
- How much improvement in these KPIs are you targeting?
- What does this improvement mean to you?
- What constraints do you experience or place on your business processes?
- What data do you have access to in your department?

What is the basis of the business case for a business analytics program? Commitment by a business stakeholder for delivering improvement in a specific business KPI is the basis for the business case. For example — "I can effect a 2x improvement in cross-sells if you can identify the top 20% clients suitable for my cross-sell messages". The concerned executive needs to own the responsibility for the metric. Otherwise the commitment is useless.

How does one develop a business case for a business analytics program? Once you have the baseline value of the specific business KPI, and the improvement commitment from the concerned stakeholder, you can begin business case development. Address fundamental questions with your stakeholder - Does the BA program get full credit for the improvement? For what duration can be credit be reckoned for? What type of on-going improvement is expected?

Also, determine what type of on-going improvement is even possible. Often, you can hope to gain major improvements in the beginning, and then only minor improvements on an on-going basis. Sometimes a BA effort is needed simply to keep the improvements in place. This adds to the cost portion of your business case. Convert the improvement in the business KPIs into cash inflows, and the cost of your BA program (first time as well as on-going) into cash outflows. Plug this into your NPV[18] or IRR[19] model.

[18] Net Present Value.

[19] Internal Rate of Return.

How does one make business analytics actionable? By inserting interventions into the organization's business process. For example, if your BA program identifies the top tier segment for a campaign, the call center application should be instrumented to use your list or your algorithm to drive its calling. This intervention must be envisioned at the program conception stage itself. Any costs, IT or management changes must be part of the BA program planning. Otherwise, the expected business improvements may not materialize.

What are political and organizational aspects to consider when proposing a BA program? Some issues to consider:

- Are you talking to the right stakeholders?
- Who else needs to be involved or bought in to make the program successful?
- What are the intentions behind funding the BA program?
- Do stakeholders have hypotheses (colloquially known as "gut feels" or political agendas they need to have confirmed?
- What happens if their favorite hypothesis is nullified by the BA findings?
- Once the improvement in KPIs becomes evident, are the stakeholders likely to attribute the improvement to the BA program, or to other factors? How will you ensure traceability? Should you design experiments with additional control groups to prove that your actions alone led to the improvements in outcomes?
- What IT support would you need? Determine that in the beginning and seek help.

What attitude should we expect from a stakeholder as regards data, decisions and BA? Do they have a data culture? Does the CEO believe in a data driven culture and the use of Business analytics for decision making? Is there an organization-wide commitment to action based on data? Do they understand that data can how things that could confirm their hypothesis or could negate it? Do they understand that sometimes what the data shows could be counterintuitive?

To what extent should we discuss specific business analytics techniques with stakeholders? Always focus discussions on business outcomes, actions, recommendations, causal factors. Occasionally, you may discuss techniques to clarify or explain. In general, keep the explanation of techniques to a minimum.

How should we respond when a stakeholder says "I knew all along all the things you are presenting." All good leaders have hypotheses that are built assiduously over their careers, taking actions and taking decisions, right and wrong. That said, all hypotheses need to stand the test of data. If our report shows what you have been feeling all along, the data confirms your hypotheses. Your action is much more solid and explainable using the analysis. Bear in mind the analysis could change over time and hence hypotheses testing is required periodically.

What is the relationship between business and strategy consulting and BA? The field of consulting (as practiced by the Big 4 and other strategy consulting companies) involves a great deal of industry know-how, industry experience, business process study, process engineering, and usage of industry best practices to help clients accomplish business goals. Over the last several years, many firms such as McKinsey have added BA as a back-end function to their consulting work. Associates located in their back-offices crunch data, prepare reports and equip front-end consultants with necessary ammunition. Some, like Deloitte, have added BA as a service offering specifically for financial services.

We see a distinct evolution of consulting companies who now want to use BA as an integral part of their offerings. Along with business process mapping, they also perform analytics on a sample of customer data or other organization data to discover insights. One consulting assignment discovered that 50% of a client's customers destroy value for a client. 20% of price changes left money on the table, because the organization did not sufficiently understand price elasticity. Such insights cannot be reached by using traditional consulting methodologies. BA is necessary.

We see BA becoming an integral part of business and strategy consulting. Those firms who get it and develop or obtain BA capabilities will be successful. Others will increasingly be disadvantaged.

Contributed by Kishore Rajgopal,
Entrepreneur, previously co-founder,
CrowdANALYTIX

Part II

Data Mining and Data Analytics

3 *Data Mining in a Nutshell*

The purpose of this chapter is to introduce the reader to the main concepts and data mining tools used in business analytics. Methods are described at a non-technical level, focusing on the idea behind the method, how it is used, advantages and limitations, and when the method is likely to be of value to business objectives.

THE GOAL IS TO TRANSFORM DATA INTO INFORMATION, AND INFORMATION INTO INSIGHT.

— Carly Fiorina (1954–)
President of Hewlett Packard, 1999–2005

3.1 *What Is Data Mining?*

Data mining is a field that combines methods from artificial intelligence, machine learning[1], statistics, and database systems. Machine learning and statistical tools are used for the purpose of learning through experience, in order to improve future performance. In the context of business analytics, data mining is sometimes referred to as "advanced analytics"[2].

[1] Machine learning is a scientific discipline concerned with the design and development of algorithms that allow computers to evolve behaviors based on empirical data, such as from sensor data or databases.

[2] We avoid referring to analytics as "simple" or "advanced" as these terms more appropriately describe the usage level of analytics.

We want machines that are able to learn for several reasons. From large amounts of data, hidden relationships and correlations can be extracted. Scenarios such as changing environments highlight the need for machines that can learn how to cope with modifying surroundings. Computer learning algorithms that are not produced by detailed human design but by automatic evolution can accommodate a constant stream of new data and information related to a task.

Data mining focuses on automatically recognizing complex patterns from data, to project likely outcomes. Learning is defined as the acquisition of knowledge or skill through experience. In data mining, we train computational methods to learn from data for the purpose of applying the knowledge to new cases.

The main challenge of data mining techniques is the ability to learn from a finite set of samples (data) and be able to generalize and produce useful output on new cases (scoring).

Within data mining, algorithms are divided into two major types of learning approaches:

Supervised learning: we know the labels or outcomes for a sample of records, and we wish to predict the outcomes of new or future records. In this case, the algorithm is trained to detect patterns that relate inputs and the outcome. This relationship is then used to predict future or new records. An example is predicting the next move in a chess game.

The fundamental approach in supervised learning is based on training the model and then evaluating its performance. Data are therefore typically segmented into three portions:

- **Training data:** the data used for training the data mining algorithm or model
- **Validation data:** used to tweak models and to compare performance across models. The rule of thumb is 80–20 for training and validation data.
- **Test data (or hold-out data):** used to evaluate the final model's performance, based on its ability to perform on new previously "unseen" data.

Unsupervised learning: we have a sample of records, each containing a set of measurements but without any particular outcome of interest. Here the goal is to detect patterns or associations that help find groups of records or relationships between measurements, to create insights about relationships between records or between measurements. An example is Amazon's recommendation system that recommends a set of products based on browsing and purchase information.

3.2 *Predictive Analytics*

This set of tools includes a wide variety of methods and algorithms from statistics and machine learning. We cover a few of the most popular predictive analytics tools. Interested

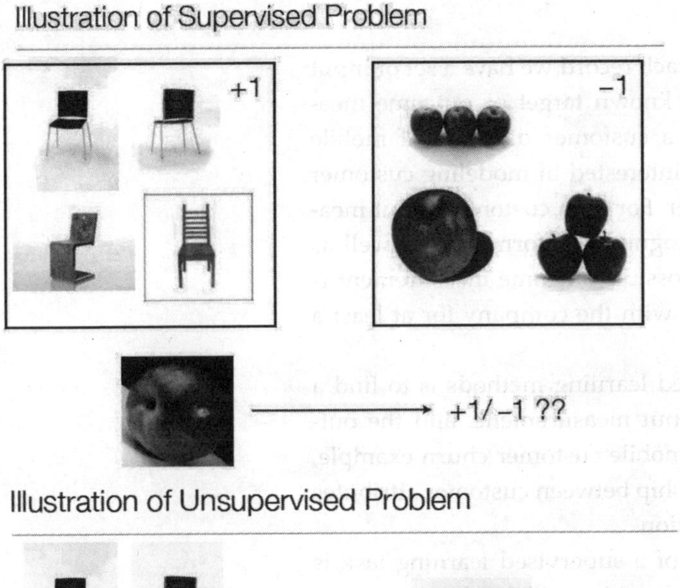

Figure 3.1: The difference between supervised and unsupervised problems. In the supervised learning task we try to classify the object as chair (+1) or an apple (−1). In the unsupervised learning case, we try to measure similarity of an item to other items.

reader can obtain information about further methods or further technical details from more specialized books.

COMPUTERS ARE USELESS. THEY CAN ONLY GIVE YOU ANSWERS.

— Pablo Picasso (1881–1973)

Supervised Learning

In supervised learning, for each record we have a set of input measurements as well as a known target or outcome measurement. For example, in a customer database of mobile phone users, where we are interested in modeling customer churn, a record is a customer. For each customer, input measurements can include demographic information as well as call and billing history. A possible outcome measurement is whether the customer stays with the company for at least a year.

The purpose of supervised learning methods is to find a relationship between the input measurements and the outcome measurement. In the mobile customer churn example, we are looking for a relationship between customer attributes and behavior and their attrition.

Another classic example of a supervised learning task is the prediction of spam (unsolicited email) for the purpose of spam filtering. Each record is an email message, for which we have multiple input measurements such as the sender address, the title, and text length. The outcome of interest is a label of "spam" or "non-spam."

In the above examples of customer churn and spam, the outcome measurement is categorical: whether a customer stays or not, or whether an email is spam or not. This type of outcome is called a *class*. Predicting the outcome is therefore called *classification*.

Supervised learning includes scenarios where the outcome measurement is either categorical or numerical. Some examples of a numerical outcome are predicting the duration of service calls at a call center based on input measurements that are available before the call is taken, or predicting the amount of cash withdrawn in each ATM transaction before the actual amount is keyed in by the customer. When the outcome is numerical, the supervised learning task is called *prediction*[3].

[3] In machine learning, the term used for predicting a numerical outcome is *regression*.

The following supervised learning techniques are used for classification and/or prediction. The various methods, each with strengths and weaknesses, approach the task of detecting potential relationships between the input and outcome measurements differently.

k-Nearest Neighbors (k-NN)

k-nearest neighbors (k-NN) algorithms are useful for both classification and prediction. They can be used to predict categorical and numerical outcomes. The algorithm identifies *k* records in the training set that are most similar to the record to be predicted, in terms of input measurements. These *k* neighbors are then used to generate a prediction of the outcome for the record of interest. If the outcome is categorical, we let the neighbors 'vote' to determine the predicted class of the record of interest. If the outcome is numerical, we simply take an average of the neighbors' outcome measurement to obtain the prediction.

The nearest neighbors approach is what real estate agents tend to instinctively use when pricing a new property. They seek similar properties in terms of size, location and other features and then use these reference properties to price the new property.

Consider the mobile customer churn example for predicting how likely a new customer is to stay with the company for at least one year. The *k*-nearest-neighbors algorithm searches the customer database for a set of *k* customers similar to the to-be-predicted customer in terms of demographic, calling and billing profiles. The algorithm then "considers" the churn behavior of the *k* neighbors and uses the most popular class (churn/no churn) to predict the class of the new customer. If we are interested in a *probability* of churn, the algorithm can compute the percentage of neighbors who churned.

In the call-center call duration example, we want to predict the duration of an incoming call before it begins. The k-NN algorithm searches the historic database for *k* calls with similar features (information available on the caller, call time, etc.). The average call duration of these *k* similar calls is then the predicted duration for the new call.

To illustrate the k-NN algorithm graphically, consider the example of predicting whether an online auction will be competitive or not. A competitive auction is one that receives more than a single bid. Using a set of over 1,000 eBay auctions, we examine two input measurements in each auction:

the seller rating (where higher ratings indicate more experience) and the opening price set by the seller.

The relationship between the auction competitiveness outcome and these two inputs is shown in Figure 3.2. Suppose that we want to predict the outcome for a new auction, given the seller rating and opening price. This new record is denoted by a question mark in the chart. The k-NN algorithm searches for the *k* nearest auctions. In this case *k* was chosen to be 7. Among the seven neighbors, five were competitive auctions; the predicted probability of this auction to be competitive is therefore 5/7. If we use a majority rule to generate a classification, then the five competitive auctions are the majority of the seven neighboring auctions, and k-NN classifies the new auction as being competitive.

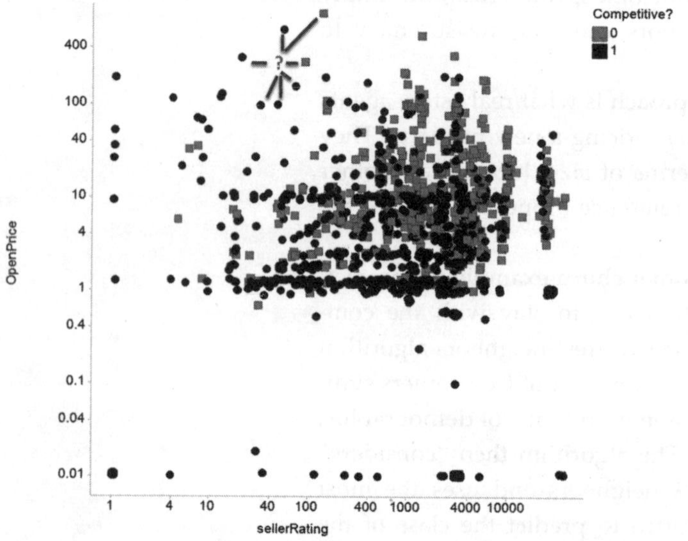

Figure 3.2: Competitive auctions (black circles) and non-competitive auctions (gray squares) as a function of seller rating and opening price in eBay auctions. k-nearest neighbors classifies a new auction's competitiveness based on *k* auctions with similar seller ratings and opening prices.

A *k*-nearest neighbors algorithm requires determining two factors: the number of neighbors to use (*k*) and the definition of similarity between records. The number of neighbors should depend on the nature of the relationship between the input and outcome measurements in terms of its global versus local nature. In a global pattern, the same relationship holds across all input values, whereas in local patterns different relationships exist for different values of the input values.

In the mobile churn example, if churn decreases in age regardless of other demographics or billing features, then we can say that there is a global relationship between churn and age. However, if churn decreases in age only for heavy callers but increases for low-volume callers, then the relationship between churn and age is local. A small number of neighbors is better for capturing local relationships — only a small set of very close neighbors would be similar to the record of interest — whereas in global relationships a large number of neighbors leads to more precise predictions.

The choice of k is typically done automatically. The algorithm is run multiple times, each time varying the value of k (starting with $k = 2$) and evaluating the predictive accuracy on a validation set. The number of neighbors that produces the most accurate predictions on the validation set is chosen.

Similarity between records can be determined in many ways. Records are compared in terms of their input measurements. The similarity metric most commonly used in k-NN algorithms is Euclidean distance. To measure the distance between two records, we look at each input measurement separately and measure the squared difference between the two records. We then take a sum of all the squared differences across the various input measurements. This is the Euclidean distance between two records.

For example, the Euclidean distance between two auctions is computed by summing up the squared difference between the pair of seller ratings and the squared difference between the pair of opening prices. You may have noticed that computing a Euclidean distance in this way will produce a similarity measure that gives much more weight to input measurements with large scales (such as seller ratings, compared to opening prices). For this reason, it is essential to first normalize the input measurements before computing Euclidean distances. Normalizing can be done in different ways. Two common normalizing approaches are converting all scales to a [0,1] scale or subtracting the mean and dividing by the standard deviation. While similarity between records can be measured in different ways, Euclidean distance is appealing because of its computational efficiency.

In k-NN, computational efficiency is especially important because the algorithm computes the similarity between the to-be-predicted record with each and every record in the training data. Moreover, if we want to predict many new records (such as for a large set of potential customers), the computational task can be heavy.

The Verdict: Among supervised learning methods, k-NN is simple to explain and easy to automate. It can be used for both prediction and classification and is highly data-driven, i.e., there are no assumptions about the nature of the relationship between the outcome and inputs. While k-NN is simple to explain, it produces "black-box" predictions because it is not clear which inputs contribute to the prediction and to what degree. When transparency is needed, k-NN is not an appealing candidate.

One key requirement of k-NN algorithms is sufficient training data. k-NN must be able to find a sufficient number of close neighbors to produce accurate predictions. Unfortunately, the number of required records increases exponentially in the number of input measurements, a problem called "the curse of dimensionality". Another challenge that KNN faces is computational: the time to find the nearest neighbors in a large training dataset can be prohibitive. While there are various tricks to try to address the curse of dimensionality and the computational burden, these two issues must be considered as inherent challenges within k-NN.

Classification and Regression Trees (CART)

Classification and regression trees are supervised learning algorithms that can be used for both classification ("classification trees") and prediction ("regression trees"). Like k-NN, the idea is to define neighborhoods of similar records, and to use those neighborhoods to produce predictions or classifications for new records. However, the way that trees determine neighborhoods is very different from k-NN. In particular, trees create *rules* that split data into different zones based on input measurements, so that each zone is dominated by records with a similar outcome. In the eBay auctions example, we might have a rule that says "IF the opening price is below $1 AND the seller rating is above 100, THEN the auction is competitive."

To create rules, tree algorithms sequentially split input predictors into two ranges: above and below some value. The algorithm starts by looking for the best split, one that produces two sets of records that are each as homogeneous as possible in terms of the outcome. Finding the best split requires trying different values across all the different input measurements. Once the first split is determined, the algorithm searches for another split, which will further break down the two data groups into three sets. The next step is finding a third split, and so forth.

The splitting process is illustrated graphically in Figure 3.3 for two input measurements, using the eBay auctions example. The first split uses the opening price, and creates two zones: above and below \$1.23. We can see that the lower zone is dominated by competitive auctions, while the upper zone is more balanced, but contains more non-competitive auctions. The second split further separates the high opening price zone (above \$1.23) by seller rating, with a high seller rating zone (above 300) and a low seller zone (300 or below). This second split breaks down the upper zone into two strips, one with mostly competitive auctions and the other with mostly non-competitive auctions. The third split separates the "high opening price, high seller rating" zone further, by seller rating (above/below \$5).

Displaying the results in a scatter plot with splits as in Figure 3.3 is no longer possible once additional input measurements are introduced. However, there is an alternative powerful chart that can be used to display the resulting splits, in the form of a tree. The tree for this same example is shown in Figure 3.4. Starting from top to bottom, each layer of the tree represents a split, in the order it occurred. The rectangles are called "leaf nodes" or "terminal nodes", and they represent the outcome of the records that fall in that zone. For example, 89% of the auctions with an opening price below \$1.23 are competitive (as can be seen in Figure 3.4).

To convert the leaf node probabilities to competitive/non-competitive classifications, we specify a majority threshold. The default threshold of 50% means that a leaf node with fewer than 50% competitive auctions will lead to a non-competitive classification (such as the right-most leaf node in Figure 3.4), whereas a leaf node with 50% or more competitive auctions will lead to a competitive classification. For a numerical outcome, such as call duration, the leaf node label is typically the average outcome of records in that leaf node.

A tree can easily be translated into a set of logical rules that relate the outcome of interest to the input measurements. In our example, using a 50% majority threshold, we have four rules:

1. IF the opening price is below \$1.23, THEN the auction is competitive.

2. IF the opening price is above \$1.23, AND the seller rating is below 300, THEN the auction is competitive.

3. IF the opening price is above \$1.23, AND the seller rating is above 300, AND the opening price is below \$5, THEN

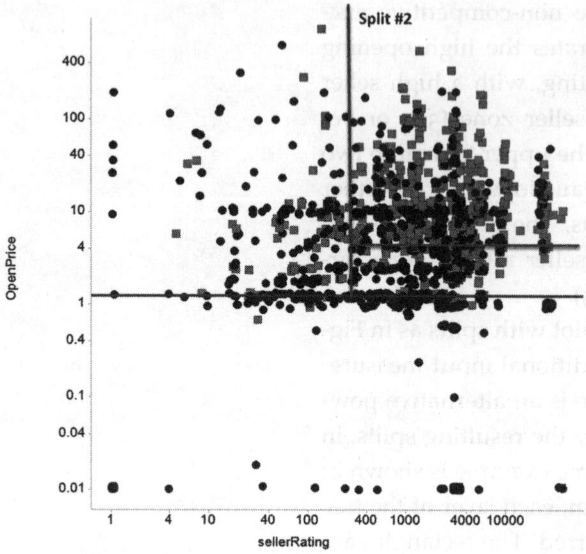

Figure 3.3: Competitive auctions (black circles) and non-competitive auctions (grey squares) as a function of seller rating and opening price in eBay auctions. The classification tree splits the auctions first by opening price (above/below$1.23), then the high opening price zone is split by seller rating above/below 300, and then the high seller rating zone is further split by opening price (above/below $5). Each of the four zones has a majority of auctions with similar outcomes (competitive/non-competitive).

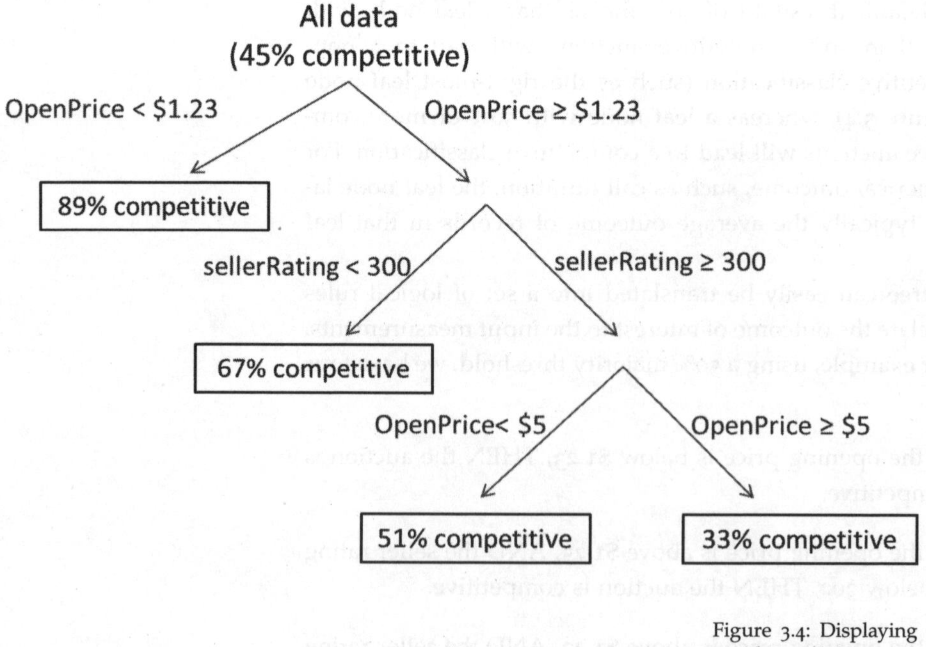

Figure 3.4: Displaying the algorithm splitting results in the form of a tree.

the auction is competitive.

4. IF the opening price is above $1.23, AND the seller rating is above 300, AND the opening price is above $5, THEN the auction is non-competitive.

Obviously, these rules can be further compressed into a smaller set of rules ("IF the opening price is above $5 AND the seller rating is above 300, THEN the auction is non-competitive; otherwise it is competitive").

Using a tree to generate predictions or classifications is straightforward: simply drop a new record at the top of the tree and find out in which leaf node it lands. The leaf node then determines the class or prediction for that record.

The two factors that must be determined in a tree algorithm are the function measuring homogeneity of a set of records in terms of the outcome, and the size of the tree in terms of splits. Typical homogeneity measures are the famous Gini index for classification tasks, and the standard deviation for prediction tasks. Most software packages will have defaults and some allow users to choose between different homogeneity measures.

Determining tree size is an important step. Too many splits result in over-fitting the training data. An extreme example is when each zone contains a single class. This will typically require many splits and the final zone will contain very few records. Most tree algorithms use an automated approach, where validation data are used to determine the tree size, thereby avoiding over-fitting. A tree that produces predictions on the training data that are much more accurate than predictions on the validation data is clearly over-fitting. Algorithms are designed to avoid this scenario.

The Verdict: CART has proven useful in a wide range of business applications. Its biggest strength among data-driven algorithms is transparency and interpretability. The ability to understand the relationship between a prediction and the input measurements is crucial in applications such as insurance underwriting, as well as for increasing the comfort level of users who are not analytics-savvy. Trees are often used in applications with a large number of potential input measurements, for the purpose of ranking the importance of the input measurements.

Trees are highly automated. They do not require any user input, and do not make assumptions about the type of relationship between the outcome and input measurements. Because of their data-driven nature, they require a large number of records for training, and a separate set for validation. Trees are robust to extreme records, and can be applied to data with missing values. However, a small change in the data can result in a different tree. In terms of computation, trees can be computationally expensive, increasingly so as the number of input measurements increases.

Finally, extensions of trees such as *random forests* and *boosted trees* improve prediction accuracy and stability. These extensions are based on creating multiple trees from the data and combining them to produce better predictions.

Regression Models

CART and k-NN are both data-driven algorithms, where users need not specify the form of the relationship between the outcome and the input measurements. These methods therefore require large amounts of training data, and are subject to over-fitting. A different approach is to model the relationship between the outcome and input measurements via a statistical model of the form:

$$Outcome = \beta_0 + \beta_1 \times Input_1 + \beta_2 \times Input_2 + \ldots$$

We call this type of model a *regression model*.

Consider the example of a car manufacturer interested in predicting the cost of the three-year warranty it provides to customers. The manufacturer has access to a large dataset of historical warranty claims, with detailed information on each claim. The challenge is to determine which input measurements are predictive of warranty cost and how to use this information to predict the warranty cost for new cars. Figure 3.5 illustrates a regression model for modeling the relationship between the warranty cost (outcome) and the vehicle odometer reading (single input measurement)[4]. The straight line denotes the regression equation, and we see that the specific regression formula estimated from the training data is:

$$\text{Warranty Cost} = 174.45 + 0.01 \times \text{Odometer Reading},$$

where cost is in USD and odometer reading is in miles. The regression tells us that the higher the odometer reading, the higher the warranty cost. Moreover, each additional mile on the odometer increases the predicted cost by one cent ($0.01). While it is difficult to display a model of warranty cost on more than a single input measurement using a chart, regression models do scale up to cases of multiple input measurements.

[4] The data for this illustration is a sample from the "Don't Get Kicked" competition on www.kaggle.com.

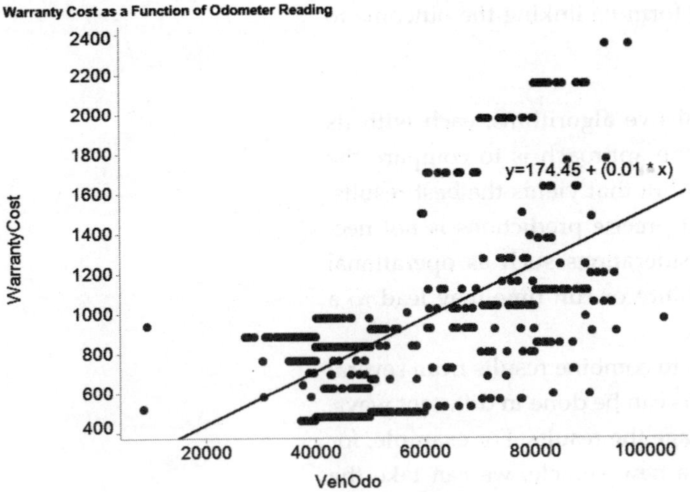

Figure 3.5: A regression model for predicting warranty cost of a vehicle by its odometer reading. Each point corresponds to a vehicle.

Although a linear relationship is a rough approximation of a more complicated relationship, it may be sufficient for producing sufficiently accurate predictions. Moreover, variations of the linear model above can yield input-outcome functions that are non-linear, such as exponential or polynomial. For a categorical outcome with two or more classes, regression formulas are available that link class probability with the inputs. A popular regression model for a categorical outcome is the logistic regression model.

By specifying a mathematical function that relates outcome to input measurements, we significantly reduce the computational burden and use the data more efficiently. Rather than using the data to detect the relationship structure, we specify the structure and use the data only to estimate the function parameters ($\beta_0, \beta_1, \beta_2, \ldots$).

The Verdict: Regression models are popular predictive tools. They can be used for classification and prediction and can capture linear, non-linear or any pre-specified relationship functions between the outcome and input measurements. In addition to providing predictions, regression models also provide information about the importance of different input measurements through quantifiable coefficients (β values). Like CART, regression models are considered transparent and interpretable. They do not require large amounts of training data. By pre-specifying an approximate formula (such as a linear function) smaller amounts of data are needed. The main weakness of regression models is the need for users to specify the formula linking the outcome to the inputs.

Ensembles

Given the variety of predictive algorithms, each with its strengths and weaknesses, one approach is to compare the results and choose the algorithm that yields the best results. The algorithm with the most precise predictions is not necessarily the best. Other considerations such as operational costs, future software availability or run time may lead to a different choice of algorithm.

An alternative approach is to combine results from several algorithms. Combining results can be done in different ways. A simple approach is to average the results. For example, for predicting warranty cost of a new vehicle, we can take the average of the cost predictions generated by different algorithms. For a classification task such as churn/no-churn, we can classify a new customer by a majority vote of class predictions by different algorithms.

The averaging or voting operations are easily automated, thereby producing a hybrid algorithm, typically called an ensemble. Ensembles rely on the same principle as diversified financial portfolios: they reduce risk. In the context of prediction, this means that ensembles produce more precise predictions. This phenomenon has been demonstrated in many real world cases. Ensembles played a major role in the million-dollar Netflix Prize contest[5], where teams competed in creating the most accurate predictions of movie preferences by users of the Netflix DVD rental service. Different teams ended up joining forces to create ensemble predictions, which proved more accurate than the individual predictions. The winning "BellKor's Pragmatic Chaos" team combined results from the "BellKor" and "Big Chaos" teams and additional members. In a 2010 article in *Chance magazine*, the Netflix Prize winners described the power of their ensemble approach [2]:

[5] www.netflixprize.com

> An early lesson of the competition was the value of combining sets of predictions from multiple models or algorithms. If two prediction sets achieved similar RMSEs, it was quicker and more effective to simply average the two sets than to try to develop a new model that incorporated the best of each method. Even if the RMSE for one set was much worse than the other, there was almost certainly a linear combination that improved on the better set.

Another way to create ensembles is to split the data into

multiple sub-samples, to run a particular algorithm separately on each sample, and then to combine the results. There are also various ways to combine results. For example, instead of an average we can take a weighted average that gives more weight to more precise predictions. Lastly, some data mining algorithms are themselves ensembles. For example, *random forests* are an ensemble of classification or regression trees.

The Verdict: Ensembles, or combining algorithm results, is a useful way to generate more precise and more robust predictions. The only caveat with the ensemble approach is that it requires more resources than a single algorithm. It requires running each of the algorithms at the production stage and whenever new predictions are needed. Constraints such as run time or future software availability should therefore be carefully considered.

Unsupervised Learning

In unsupervised learning, we have a set of measurements for each record. As in supervised learning, it is important to define what is a record, because different definitions will lead to different data structures. For example, from a bank's database we can extract a dataset of customers, where a set of measurements is available for each customer: demographic information, banking history (number of monthly ATM transactions, teller transactions, loans, etc.). Alternatively, we can extract a dataset of single transactions, where measurements are given on each transaction (time of day, type of transaction, amount, etc.). A third option is to define a record as a teller encounter, where measurements are the types of products or services rendered in that encounter as well as the customer data.

The purpose of unsupervised learning methods is to find relationships either between measurements or between records. Note that in contrast to supervised learning, we do not differentiate between input and outcome measurements. In the bank customer dataset, for instance, we might be interested in discovering different types of customers in terms of their banking history. This popular task is called *customer segmentation*. In the teller encounter example, we might want to learn which products/services tend to go together, for purposes such as providing product recommendations, determining marketing campaigns, etc. Several algorithms are popular for these various tasks, ranging from *collaborative filtering* methods to *market basket analysis*.

A third relationship of interest is figuring out the amount of information overlap in a large set of measurements, usually in an effort to reduce the number of measurements to a smaller, more manageable one. This process is called *dimension reduction*. In the following sections we describe several popular unsupervised data mining techniques.

Cluster Analysis (Segmentation)

Cluster analysis is an exploratory tool for discovering clusters of similar records. Humans can easily detect similarities and differences between objects in some contexts. For example, we easily distinguish between a cat and a dog, despite the fact that they share many common features (four legs, fur, etc.). Yet, when it comes to many rows of records with multiple measurements, our ability to find similarities and differences between records is challenged.

Clustering algorithms are an automated way of detecting clusters of similar records. Similarity requires defining a metric that compares all the measurements of interest. For example, the similarity between two bank accounts can be measured by comparing the different features of the two accounts such as account type, recent activity, current balance, etc. Various distance metrics, each with advantages and shortcomings, are used to measure the difference between a pair of records.

A popular metric is Euclidean distance, which aggregates the squared difference for each feature (we have discussed this metric earlier in the context of k-NN). For example, bank account #1 has a current balance of $2,500 and the most recent activity is 24 hours ago. Account #2 has a current balance of $3,000 and the most recent activity is 14 hours ago. The Euclidean distance between accounts #1 and #2 is $(2,500 - 3,000)^2 + (24 - 14)^2 = 250,100$. Note that using Euclidean distance requires re-scaling (normalizing) all features so that they have the same scale. Otherwise, features that have units with a wide range, such as *current balance*, will dominate the distance.

Figure 3.6 graphically illustrates the notion of clustering. The chart compares 821 vehicle records, each represented by a horizontal line (row). For each vehicle, we have four features (from left to right: odometer reading, acquisition cost, whether the vehicle was purchased online, and warranty price). The chart uses color to denote the value on each feature, so that darker color corresponds to higher values. We sorted the vehicles by odometer reading, from high to low. On this chart, we can visually detect a few types of vehicles. At the very top are "high-mileage-inexpensive-online-purchased-low-warranty-cost vehicles." At the bottom of the chart we can spot a cluster of vehicles with very low odometer readings, acquisition costs, and warranty costs. Most vehicles were purchased offline (one cluster) and a few online (another cluster).

Note how difficult it is to clearly separate the 821 vehicles into clear-cut clusters based on all four features. For this reason, data mining algorithms are needed. The result of applying a clustering algorithm is shown in Figure 3.7. The algorithm detected four clusters (labeled 10, 6, 8, 9). Clusters 10 and 6 comprise the vehicles that were purchased offline. The main difference between the clusters is the higher warranty cost and odometer readings in cluster 10.

The Verdict: We can think of cluster analysis as a way for compressing rows of a dataset. Cluster analysis is a useful approach for exploring groupings of records, based on a set of measurements. It is especially advantageous in Big Data, where the number of records and the number and variety of measurements is large.

Some clustering algorithms are designed for very large datasets and can be deployed for high-performance implementation. Note that cluster analysis is an exploratory approach. There are no correct or incorrect results. The key question is always whether the resulting clusters offer insights or lead to insightful decisions. Segmenting records into clusters is useful for various reasons and applications, including differentiated customer targeting (customary in marketing campaigns), deploying different policies to different segments (as in credit card scoring), and more.

Dimension Reduction

One feature of Big Data is the large number of measurements for each record. This richness is the result of the proliferation of digitized data collection mechanisms, including scanners, RFID readers, GPS devices and automated recording of online and mobile footprints. While more measurements may increase the richness of data, they also add a lot of noise due to errors and other factors. Moreover, measure-

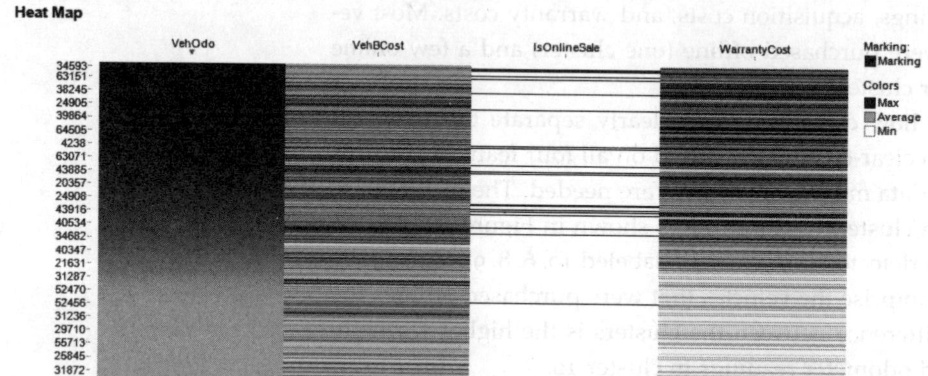

Figure 3.6: Heatmap comparing 821 vehicle records (rows) across four features. Darker color denotes higher values.

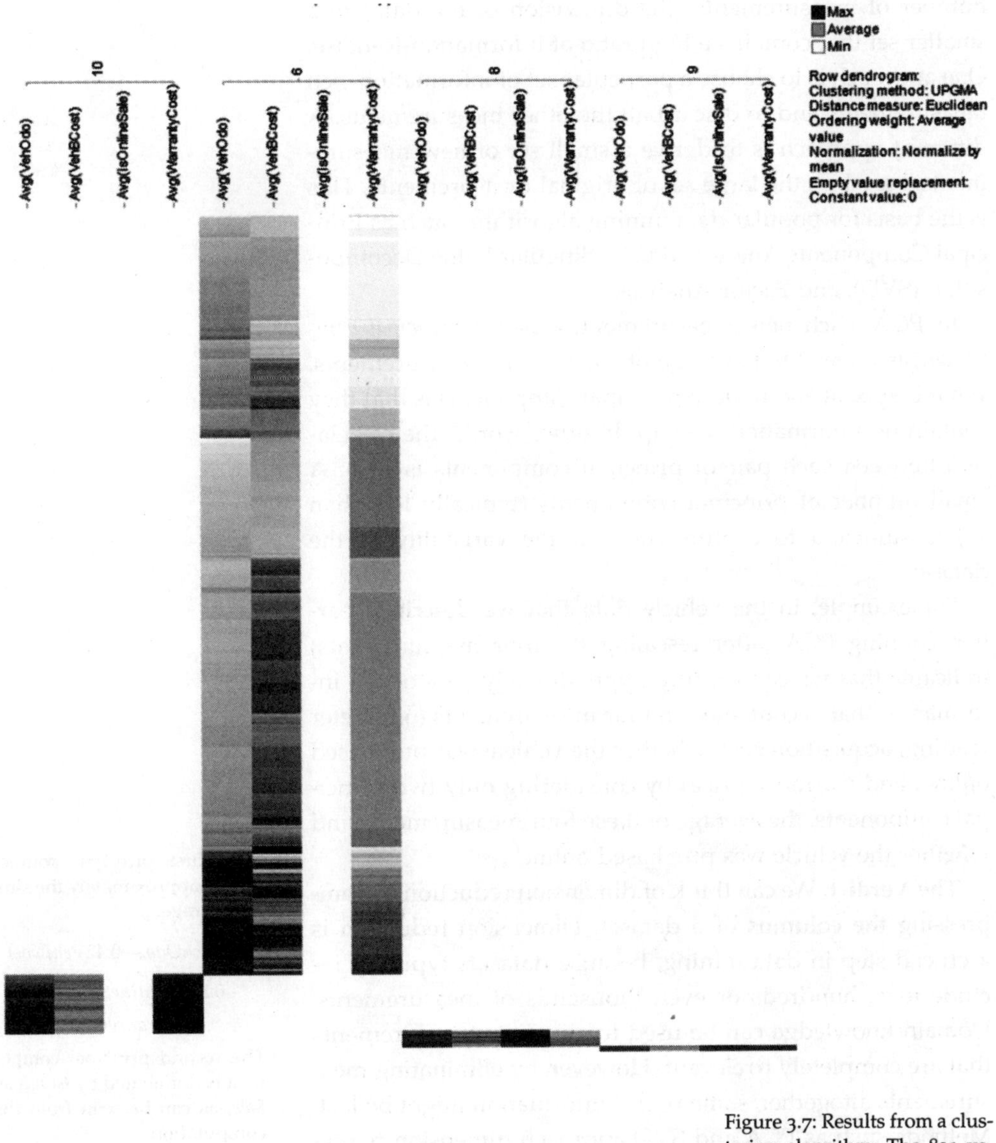

Figure 3.7: Results from a clustering algorithm: The 821 vehicle records are grouped into four clusters.

ments often contain an overlap of information. For example, *age* and *years since opening bank account* are likely to be highly correlated. The challenge is to determine what part of the data contains the information and to separate it out from the noise.

Dimension reduction techniques are aimed at reducing the number of measurements (the dimension of the data) to a smaller set that contains a high ratio of information-to-noise. One approach is to choose a particular set of information-rich measurements and to discard all the other measurements. A different approach is to derive a small set of new measurements, based on the large set of original measurements. This is the basis for popular data mining algorithms such as Principal Components Analysis (PCA), Singular Value Decomposition (SVD), and Factor Analysis.

In PCA, each new measurement, called a *principal component,* is a weighted average of the original measurements. What is special about these principal components is that they contain no information overlap. In other words, the correlation between each pair of principal components is zero. A small number of principal components (typically less than 10) is sufficient to capture most of the variability in the dataset.

For example, in the vehicle data that we described earlier, running PCA (after rescaling the four measurements) indicates that we can capture approximately 70% of the information that is contained in four measurements (odometer reading, acquisition cost, whether the vehicle was purchased online, and warranty price) by considering only two principal components: the average of these four measurements and whether the vehicle was purchased online[6].

The Verdict: We can think of dimension reduction as compressing the columns of a dataset. Dimension reduction is a crucial step in data mining, because datasets typically include tens, hundreds or even thousands of measurements. Domain knowledge can be used to eliminate measurements that are completely irrelevant. However, by eliminating measurements altogether, some useful information might be lost. Methods such as PCA and SVD approach dimension reduction in a different fashion. They help reduce information overlaps between measurements by creating a smaller set of variables that do not have information overlap. The resulting set of variables is smaller than the original set of measurements, and therefore easier to handle and faster to run

[6] The first principal component is approximately the simple average:

$$0.63 VehOdo + 0.42 VehBcost$$
$$+0.30 IsOnlineSale + 0.58$$
$$WarrantyCost.$$

The second principal component is dominated by *IsOnlineSale*, as can be seen from the computation

$$0.02 VehOdo + 0.47 VehBcost$$
$$-0.88 IsOnlineSale$$
$$+0.08 WarrantyCost.$$

in other analyses. However, computing these new variables usually requires access to the entire set of original measurements.

Association Rules (Market-Basket Analysis)

Scanners and online shopping create records of customers' "baskets." Each transaction includes a combination of products that are linked to the same record in a single transaction. Services such as movie rentals and telecom plans similarly have baskets for different customers: a basket of movies rented within the same transaction; a basket of mobile telecom services (such as a monthly 300-minute talk time, unlimited SMS and unlimited data). Similar data structures arise in healthcare: a doctor visit produces a combination of symptom data; a hospitalization produces a combination of medical procedures and tests. Online education produces data on groups of courses taken by a student.

Unlike the data structure that we described earlier, where we have a set of measurements (columns) on a set of records (rows), here different records have different measurements. If we think of baskets as records, then different baskets contain different items. This data structure is illustrated in Table 3.2, which shows an example for a fictitious pizza delivery service.

We see that different orders contain a different number of items. We could potentially restructure the data so that each item on the menu is a column and then we would list the item count for each order. However, when there are many different possible items (many SKUs in a grocery store, many possible symptoms, etc.) the latter data structure will contain mostly zeros. Association rules are an algorithm that is designed especially for such circumstances, i.e., a large set of potential items.

Order No.	Item 1	Item 2	Item 3	Item 4
1	Large Margherita Pizza	2-Liter Pepsi	Small salad	
2	Small Veg Pizza	Small Hawaiian Pizza		
3	Large Margherita Pizza	Large Margherita Pizza	2-Liter Pepsi	2-Liter Pepsi
4	Large salad	Small Veg Pizza		

The purpose of association rules algorithms is to discover relationships between items that co-appear in baskets, in very large transactional datasets. The algorithm does this by searching for large sets of baskets that contain the same item combinations. The result is a set of statements about which item goes with which other items. More accurately, association rules generate IF/THEN rules such as "IF Tylenol, THEN Kleenex."

In the pizza example, discovering a rule such as "IF Large Margherita THEN 2-Liter Pepsi" can be used for coupon offers, discount bundles, stocking, and designing the menu. In other words, the rules are useful for generating common, impersonal decisions.

The Verdict: Association rules are useful for discovering relationships between measurements or items in large datasets. "Large" refers to the number of records as well as to a large number of potential items. The resulting association rules are easy to understand. However, two notes of caution are in place:

- With a large dataset, association rules will produce a large number of rules. One danger is "discovering" rules that do not generalize and instead reflect combinations that are simply due to chance.
- Discovered rules can be uninteresting or trivial. For example, discovering that bananas are purchased with many other products in grocery stores in the United States is unsurprizing, because bananas are a typical loss item that is offered to lure customers.

While association rules originated from grocery store transactional databases, they can be used in many other contexts and applications, including healthcare, finance, education, telecom, and more. Using association rules requires a large number of baskets and potential items, and stakeholder commitment toward generating common rules.

Collaborative Filtering

Recommender systems are common in almost every domain. They are used for book recommendations on Amazon.com, for music recommendations on personalized radio stations such as LastFM.com and on video sharing sites such as YouTube, for product recommendations in online shopping, and more.

Collaborative filtering is the algorithm behind many online recommender systems. Like association rules, collaborative filtering uses large datasets on baskets that are combinations of products or services that are consumed or purchased together. However, unlike association rules that generate general, impersonal rules, collaborative filtering generates personalized recommendations. The idea is to generate user-specific associations based on information from many other users. The fundamental assumption is that if users rate items similarly, or have similar behaviors (e.g., buying, watching, listening), they will rate or behave similarly on other items [20].

Another difference is that association rules look for popular combinations in the sense that the combinations appear many times in the dataset. In contrast, recommender systems look for combinations that are frequent among baskets that have at least one of the items, regardless of how many such baskets there are. This means that association rules ignore non-popular items while recommender systems do not. These non-popular items are what is known as "the long tail."

Collaborative filtering algorithms search for items that have a large percentage of baskets in common. In the pizza example in Table 3.2, a 2-liter Pepsi and a large pizza Margherita share 100% of the baskets that contain either a 2-liter Pepsi or a large pizza Margherita. Even if these are the only two orders in thousands of orders, this coupling will be captured by the collaborative filtering algorithm. When a new order is placed and one of these two items is mentioned, a recommendation of the second item will automatically be generated.

Another difference between association rules and collaborative filtering is in terms of implementation. Association rule algorithms are run retrospectively on a large transactional dataset, and generate rules. The rules are then used in the decision making process for purposes of generating business rules. In contrast, collaborative filtering is run on a "live" and incrementally growing dataset, and generates real-time recommendations to the end users.

The data used in recommendation systems can be user ratings of different items, which require user input. For example, Netflix solicits movie ratings from its users in order to provide them with recommendations. User preference data may also be implicit, as in purchase or consumption of item combinations. An example is book orders on Amazon.com. When ratings are used, user-based collaborative filtering algorithms search for users who rate a set of items similarly and use this group as "neighbors" to generate recommendations for a new similar user. This is the same idea as the k-NN algorithm (Section 3.2), where the predictors are ratings of items and the outcome is an item not yet rated by the user but rated by neighbors.

Another type of collaborative filtering is item-based. In this case "similarity" refers to items, so that items with similar user ratings or those purchased together are considered similar. This approach is the basis for Amazon.com's recommender system that produces recommendations of the type "Customers who bought this item also bought...."

A major challenge with collaborative filtering is that most users (rows) only have values or ratings on a small number of items. The resulting users-by-items dataset therefore typically has many missing values. This "sparsity" issue poses various challenges. Because similarity is based on common items (which may be relatively rare), results can be unreliable. One approach to dealing with the many missing values is applying dimension reduction methods.

The Verdict: The personalized nature of collaborative filtering recommendations, and the possibility of implementing them in real-time, makes them desirable techniques for online or other real-time recommendation systems. We noted the sparsity issues, for which various solutions are available. Two conceptual limitations to consider are the lack of recommendations for users who are dissimilar from all other users and the reliance of similarity on combinations of behaviors but not on combinations of non-behaviors (such as the absence of certain symptom combinations). In spite of the above, collaborative filtering is considered one of the most successful recommender system techniques.

3.3 *Forecasting*

The term *forecasting* commonly refers to prediction of future values. While it is similar to supervised learning as described in Section 3.2, forecasting has a few distinguishing features. The first characteristic is the type of data. In forecasting, the outcome measurement is usually a series of values over time, called a *time series*. Examples include data on quarterly sales, average daily temperature, hourly website traffic, and annual rainfall. Second, the typical goal is to generate a forecast of future values of the time series. For example, forecasting demand in the next four quarters or forecasting weekly stock-outs.

The main assumption underlying forecasting techniques is that behaviors and patterns observed in the past will continue in the future. For example, an increasing trend is expected to increase further in the future. A seasonal pattern will recur in the future. The equivalent of this assumption in the ordinary supervised learning context is that the existing data are similar to the new data that will be scored/predicted.

While the supervised learning methods can be used for forecasting, the temporal nature of both data and goal requires modifications. Let us consider a few key modifications.

Outcome and Input Measurements

Two forecasting approaches are extrapolation and causal regression. Extrapolation techniques use early measurements of the series as input measurements for later measurements (the outcome). Supervised learning methods such as regression can then be applied to the input and output columns. When the series contains a trend and/or seasonal cycles, special input measurements are created to capture such patterns. For example, to capture a linear trend of an annual demand series, we can model the demand values (the outcome) in a linear regression with the column of year numbers as an input variable.

In addition to the input measurements based on the series' past, additional external information can be included as input variables, similar to ordinary supervised learning

Asur and Huberman [7] created a forecasting model for box-office revenue generated by a movie in its opening weekend. Their input variables are based on tweets (posts on Twitter.com) that referred to the movie prior to its release. To forecast box-office revenue for a particular movie in its opening weekend, they used the "daily tweet ratio" from each of the last seven days as seven input variables.

[7] S. Asur and B. A. Huberman. Predicting the future with social media. *IEEE/WIC/ACM International Conference on Web Intelligence and Intelligent Agent Technolgy*, pages 492–499, 2010.

Training and Holdout Data

In Section 3.2 we introduced the practice of partitioning the data into training, validation and test portions in order to evaluate the predictive accuracy of a solution on new data. In the case of time series, we cannot use random segmentation, because it will create "holes" in the series. The values in a time series are ordered chronologically and this order is of importance. Therefore, the concept of data partitioning is carried out by splitting the series into an earlier training period and a later validation period (the most recent portion of the series) that is considered the holdout period.

Data mining algorithms are trained on the training period and their performance is evaluated on the holdout period. The holdout period is the future, relative to the training period. Determining where to split the series depends on different aspects of the forecasting goal and the nature of the data, such as the forecast horizon and the types of patterns that the data exhibit. Time series partitioning is illustrated in Figure 3.8.

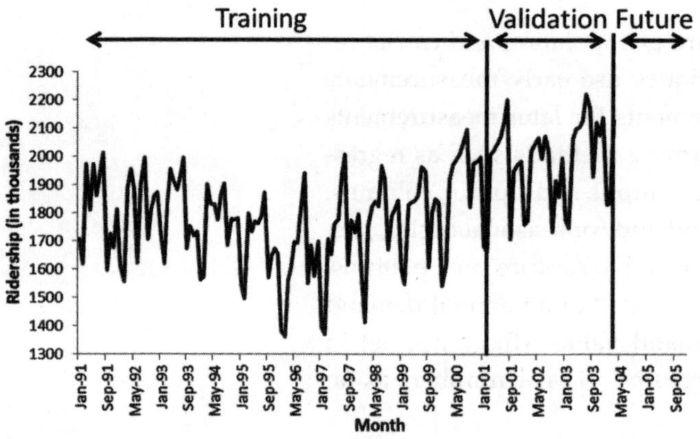

Figure 3.8: Illustration of partitioning a time series into training and holdout periods (from G. Shmueli. *Practical Time Series Forecasting: A Hands-On Guide*. CreateSpace, 2nd edition, 2011, with permission).

Further Forecasting Methods

The temporal nature of a time series usually implies correlation between neighboring values (*autocorrelation*). This also implies that the most recent values in a series carry the freshest information for forecasting future values. There are various techniques that approach the forecasting task by directly capturing this fact. The simplest are smoothing methods, such as the *moving average* and *exponential smoothing*. A moving average produces forecasts by taking the average of the most recent values of the series. Exponential smoothing forecasts are a weighted average of all past values with decaying weights into the past. More sophisticated smoothing methods exist for forecasting series with trends and seasonal patterns.

A different approach that is somewhat similar to regression models is based on fitting a formula that directly models the relationship between a value and past values. Methods such as *Autoregressive Integrated Moving Average (ARIMA)* models and state space models are based on this approach. The formula can be quite complicated, and automated procedures are used to find the formula's parameters that generate the best forecasts.

Forecasting Many Series

While forecasting methods have been used for decades, a new aspect of forecasting is the need to forecast a very large number of series, sometimes in real-time. Examples include retail stores and chains that require forecasts for each Stock Keeping Unit (SKU). Websites such as Google Insights for Search produce immediate forecasts for keyword popularity according to the keywords typed by users. Farecast.com (now Bing Travel, by Microsoft `www.bing.com/travel/about/howAirPredictions.do`) produces forecasts for many air travel routes, to determine the best time to purchase air tickets. Forecasting algorithms predict whether the airfare on a certain route will increase/decrease with a certain confidence level.

In this new realm, the role of automation is critical. Algorithms that can be automated and that have low memory and storage requirements are often preferred over alternatives that might produce slightly more accurate forecasts.

The Verdict: Forecasting is an important component of supervised learning, although the temporal nature of the data and the goal require some modifications to non-temporal approaches. In addition, specialized forecasting algorithms exist that take advantage of the correlation between neighboring values in the series. Today's context often requires generating forecasts for a large number of series, often in real-time. Automated forecasting algorithms are therefore at the core of many such systems.

3.4 *Optimization*

Optimization is an important tool with origins in operations research. Operations research is the discipline of applying analytical techniques to arrive at better decisions. The primary focus of this field is to arrive at optimal or near-optimal solutions for complex decision-making problems. Optimization and simulation (see Section 3.5) are the main two tools. Optimization is aimed at finding a combination of parameters that optimizes a function of interest. For example, in online advertising we might ask what ad location, size, and color lead to maximum click-through rate.

We illustrate the process of optimization through a business example. Consider a manufacturing company that produces different types of furniture. The company would like to determine which combination of items produced in one day results in maximum profit.

As a first step, it is important to understand the landscape we wish to optimize. We have three main components: the function to optimize, the parameters, and the constraints.

Parameters (Variables)

We are interested in determining the combination of furniture item quantities to produce in a day. In this example, we consider four types of items, and plan to produce quantities x_1, x_2, x_3 and x_4 of each item, respectively. Regarding the amount produced of each item, there may be minimal requirements, such as at least one item from each type. For the sake of simplicity, let us assume that there is no required minimal quota of furniture to be produced.

The output of the optimization procedure will include the values for x_1, x_2, x_3 and x_4 that optimize the daily profit.

Costs and Constraints

In our example, we want to capture the different manufactured items as well as their respective costs and profits. Costs include labor (man hours worked) and materials. We list the labor and material requirements in Table 3.1.

We also need to capture the cost and availability of the labor and required materials. These are given in Table 3.2.

	Labor (hrs)	Metal (lbs)	Wood (ft^3)	Price ($)
Chairs	1	1	3	79
Bookcases	3	1	4	125
Bed-frames	2	1	4	109
Desks	2	1	3	94

Table 3.1: The furniture company is able to produce four different items that each have different labor and material costs. The last column lists the selling price of each item.

	Labor (hrs)	Metal (lbs)	Wood (ft^3)
Cost ($)	14	20	11
Availability	225	117	420

Table 3.2: The cost and availability of labor, metal and wood for the production of chairs, bookcases, bed-frames and desks.

Objective Function

The goal stated by the company is maximizing daily profit. Assuming that all of the produced items can be sold, the business question to be addressed is: "How many desks, chairs, bookcases and bed-frames should the company produce per day in order to achieve maximum profit?" To rephrase, how can the company maximize profit given the above constraints?

Computing profit requires computing costs and revenues. For a given set of furniture item quantities x_1, x_2, x_3 and x_4, we can compute costs, revenues and resulting profits. The spreadsheet in Figure 3.9 illustrates this computation. Ordinary cells include numbers, while highlighted cells include formulas (for example, the formula for cell F11 is shown in the function bar).

Optimization Model

The optimization model can be represented with the optimization objective

Maximize { Profit = Total Revenue − Total Cost }

with the parameters on which the decision will be made on

#Desks (x_1), #Chairs (x_2), #Bookcases (x_3), and #Bed-frames (x_4)

and the constraints (limitations) to achieve the objective

Availability of labor, metal, and wood.

This optimization problem can be solved using Excel's Solver add-in[8]. Given the spreadsheet in Figure 3.9, we can specify the objective function, parameters and constraints as shown in Figure 3.10, which yields the following solution

[8] For more examples of using Excel's Solver for optimization problems, see G. Shmueli. *Practical Time Series Forecasting: A Hands-On Guide*. CreateSpace, 2nd edition, 2011.

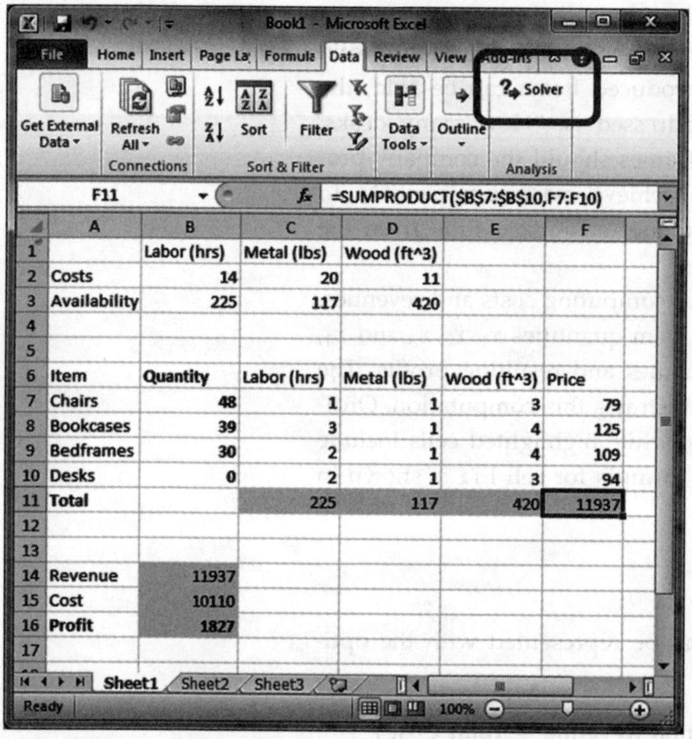

Figure 3.9: Spreadsheet with furniture example. Ordinary cells include numbers; highlighted cells include formulas. All formulas are based on the four values in the *Quantity* column.

(shown in the spreadsheet): the maximum achievable daily profit is $1827 by manufacturing 0 desks, 48 chairs, 39 bookcases and 30 bed-frames. Examining the pre-determined constraints, we find that we maximally and exactly utilize the full availability of labor at 225 hours, metal at 117 and wood at 420 with zero daily surplus.

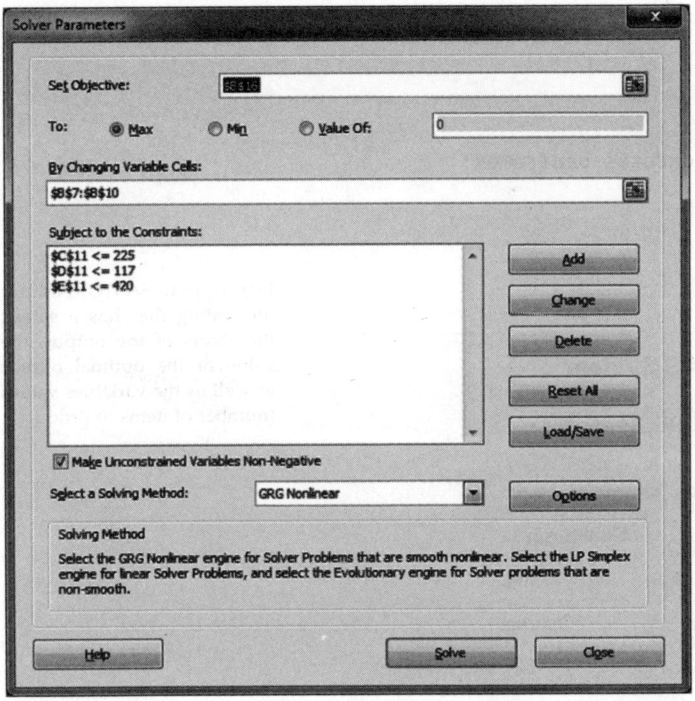

Figure 3.10: Using Excel's Solver add-in to solve the optimization problem. The optimal solution (parameters and profit) is shown in Figure 3.9 in bold.

The optimization model above, together with the information in Tables 3.1 and 3.2, can also be translated into the following optimization code[9]:

```
proc optmodel;
   /* declare variables */
   var desks >= 0, chairs >= 0, bookcases >= 0,
    bedframes >= 0;

   /* declare constraints */
   con Labor: 2*desks + 1*chairs + 3*bookcases
                      + 2*bedframes <= 225;
   con Metal: 1*desks + 1*chairs + 1*bookcases
                      + 1*bedframes <= 117;
```

[9] The code is written and executed in SAS\OR. *Optmodel* indicates that the type of optimization solver would be automatically selected.

```
con Wood: 3*desks + 3*chairs + 4*bookcases
                    + 4*bedframes <= 420;

/* declare objective */
max Profit =
    94*desks + 79*chairs + 125*bookcases + 109*bedframes
  - 14 * (2*desks + 1*chairs + 3*bookcases + 2*bedframes)
  - 20 * (1*desks + 1*chairs + 1*bookcases + 1*bedframes)
  - 11 * (3*desks + 3*chairs + 4*bookcases + 4*bedframes);

expand;
solve;
print desks chairs bookcases bedframes;
quit;
```

The SAS System

The OPTMODEL Procedure

Solution Summary	
Solver	Dual Simplex
Objective Function	Profit
Solution Status	Optimal
Objective Value	1827
Iterations	3
Primal Infeasibility	0
Dual Infeasibility	0
Bound Infeasibility	0

desks	chairs	bookcases	bedframes
0	48	39	30

Figure 3.11: SAS\OR output illustrating the chosen solver, the status of the output, the value of the optimal output as well as the variables values (number of items to produce).

Figure 3.11 gives the output of our scenario, where the system automatically detects the type of solver to be Dual Simplex.

The solution given in Figures 3.9 and 3.11 is optimal; it is not possible to do better given the current information. However, the solution might not be operationable. Assume that our manufacturer is unable to produce zero desks due to a minimum requirement of desks, or that employees are unable to work non-stop and require fixed rest periods, etc. An optimization model will provide the best possible solution (if one is available) based on the information provided. Subsequent information that needs to be taken into account (such as labor rest periods or shift changes) would need to be included in the overall formulation.

Perhaps most importantly, the optimization framework allows for examining multiple scenarios, real and potential. We can use optimization not only to identify the feasibility of current business objectives, but also to identify the outcome if changes are incorporated. For example, we can explore the maximum possible profit and quantity of manufactured furniture items if we increase/decrease the selling price, labor hours and/or the material costs. Optimization gives us the ability to identify the best possible case under varying conditions.

Optimization Methods and Algorithms

As illustrated above, the simplest case of optimization is the maximization or minimization of an objective function by systematically choosing values from within an allowed set and computing the value of the objective function. Optimization problems fall into various categories, depending on the form of the objective function and constraints.

The simplest case is a linear objective function and linear equality or inequality constraints. Our furniture example had exactly this structure: revenue was a linear function of the four item quantities and the constraints were all linear inequalities. The common optimization technique for solving such problems is *Linear Programming (LP)*.

Optimization problems are generally divided into two types of problems, convex and non-convex. Convex problems are those with a single optimal solution. The objective function has a single minimum or maximum point.

Geometrically, a function is convex if every point on a straight line joining two points on the function is also within the region. This is illustrated in Figure 3.12, where any straight line joining two points in the convex curve is within the region, whereas for the non-convex function we can create a line external to the region by connecting two points.

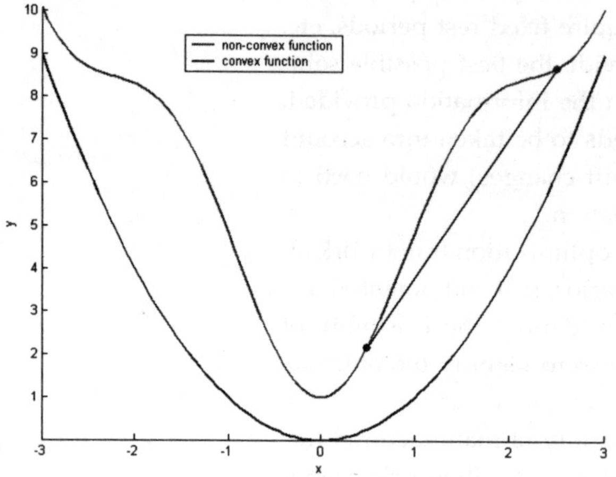

Figure 3.12: A plot of a non-convex (top line) and convex (bottom line) function. The top curve is non-convex because the black straight line segment connecting two points on the curve is below the curve ("outside the region").

In general, the difficulty of solving a problem is affected by its convexity. A variety of optimization methods exists, each designed for particular characteristics of the problem. For example, *convex programming* is used when the objective function is convex or concave (a minimization or maximization goal) and the constraint set is convex. LP is an example of convex programming. *Nonlinear programming* is needed when the objective function and/or the constraints are nonlinear.

A possible constraint is that parameter units are integers. In our furniture example, we might require the item quantities to be integers. *Integer programming* is used when some or all of the parameters are constrained to take on integer values. This is a non-convex case, and in general much more difficult than regular linear programming.

A comprehensive list of different optimization problems and methods is listed in Wikipedia's Mathematical Optimization article[10].

Many computational algorithms exist for solving optimization problems. Examples of popular algorithms include *Branch and Bound, the Expectation-Maximization (EM) Algorithm, the Genetic Algorithm,* and *the Simplex Algorithm.*[11] We note that most commercial software packages are able to automatically select the relevant technique for the defined op-

[10] en.wikipedia.org/wiki/Mathematical_optimization.

[11] For a comprehensive listing see en.wikipedia.org/wiki/Category:Optimization_algorithms_and_methods

timization problem. For a theoretical understanding of optimization methodologies see [12].

[12] Stephen Boyed and Lieven Vandenberghe. *Convex Optimization*. Cambridge University Press, 2004; R. T. Rockafellar. Lagrange multipliers and optimality. *SIAM Review*, 21(183), 1993; and T. Ui. A note on discrete convexity and local optimality. *Japan J. Indust. Appl. Math.*, 23(21), 2006.

3.5 Simulation

Simulation is a tool for scenario building and assessment, which originates in operations research and is used in a wide range of fields and applications. The purpose of simulation is to assess the impact of various factors on outcomes of interest. In particular, simulation is the process of imitating an operation of a process over time. We can then change various process parameters and conditions and see how they affect the process outcomes of interest.

Simulation and optimization are sometimes confused. The main difference is that in *optimization* we search for combinations of inputs that lead to some optimal outcome, whereas *simulation* imitates a prescribed process flow over time — it does not optimize the process.

Let us continue our example of the furniture company. We used optimization to find the optimal combination of furniture items produced daily in order to maximize profit, given various constraints. We can use simulation to assess how the optimal solution (daily production process) will be affected by factors not considered in the optimization. For example, what if we over-estimated the number of work hours? What if a large order comes in? Moreover, although we stated the different costs and requirements as figures (such as 1 hour for producing a chair), there is always some random fluctuation in these figures. For instance, a chair might take anywhere between 45 minutes and 1.5 hours to produce. We therefore may wish to *simulate* the furniture assembly line by capturing the steps required to assemble the different types of furniture. Such a simulation can help us evaluate the outcome under a broader context, taking into account random fluctuation. The simulation can help identify bottlenecks in the process as well as whether the process is sustainable over time.

Monte Carlo Simulation

One approach to incorporating random variability into the simulation is using Monte Carlo experiments. The idea behind this approach is to compute the relationship of interest multiple times, each time varying parameters according to some random process. By examining the different runs, we get an idea of possible fluctuations in the outcomes of interest and their sensitivity to changes in the parameters. In our furniture example, costs of labor and material were stated as fixed figures. Suppose that the number of hours to produce each of the furniture items can vary within half an hour of the values in Table 3.1 due to causes not under our control (differences in skill level, effects of temperature on workers, etc.). How does this extra variability affect the daily profit? How much variation does it introduce into our setup?

To take into account the above-mentioned random variation in labor time, we replace the values in cells C7:C10 in the spreadsheet shown in Figure 3.9 with a formula that adheres to the type of randomness that we envisage. If we assume that building a chair can take anywhere between half an hour and 1.5 hours, and that any value within this range is equally likely, then we can use the Excel formula *=0.5+RAND()*, where the function RAND() generates a random number between 0 and 1. Figure 3.13 shows the result of a single run. We see that the RAND() functions that were inserted into the labor values lead to a slightly different daily profit. Compared to the original profit of $1,827, the profit in this screenshot is $1,918. However, this is only a single run, representing one possible outcome. In Excel, we can regenerate random numbers by pressing the F9 key. The next step is to aggregate the results from multiple runs, and to examine the variation in profit across the different runs. This is typically done by examining a chart of profit across the different runs. An example is shown in Figure 3.14, where we see the likelihood of obtaining different profit levels.

In short, simulation helps us assess the uncertainty associated with the relationship between the process parameters and the objectives. Monte Carlo simulation does this by adding random variation into the process parameters. In this example, we chose a uniform distribution (function RND()) to represent the randomness structure. However, many other probability distributions can be used instead.

Let us expand on our previous example and assume that the furniture company also provides repair and maintenance services for the items it manufactures. We would now want to know whether the current inventory holding level sufficiently adheres to the company's service agreements, which target a certain customer service level. Suppose that the company requires a 95% service level, where 95% of all spare

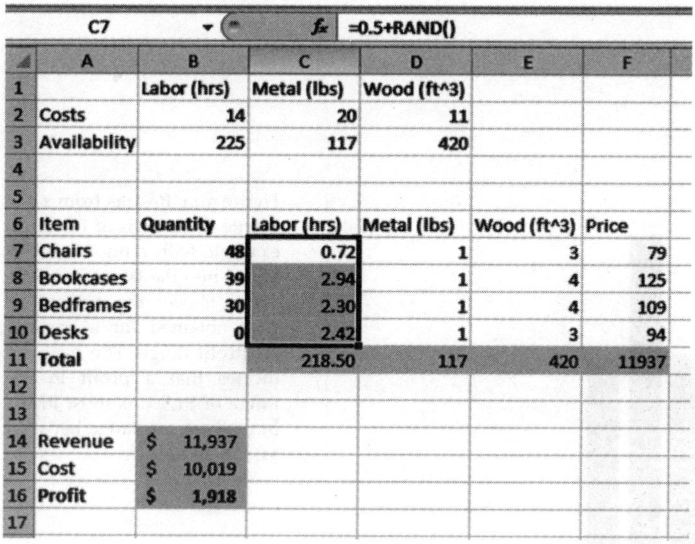
C7 fx =0.5+RAND()

	A	B	C	D	E	F
1		Labor (hrs)	Metal (lbs)	Wood (ft^3)		
2	Costs	14	20	11		
3	Availability	225	117	420		
4						
5						
6	Item	Quantity	Labor (hrs)	Metal (lbs)	Wood (ft^3)	Price
7	Chairs	48	0.72	1	3	79
8	Bookcases	39	2.94	1	4	125
9	Bedframes	30	2.30	1	4	109
10	Desks	0	2.42	1	3	94
11	Total		218.50	117	420	11937
12						
13						
14	Revenue	$ 11,937				
15	Cost	$ 10,019				
16	Profit	$ 1,918				
17						

Figure 3.13: Furniture example with randomness inserted into the labor time (cells C7:C10). The effect can be seen on the revenue, cost, and profit values.

parts are available at all times, while the remaining 5% require special order or are on queue for repair. We simulate the demand for repair parts, assuming that each part is completely repairable.

Let us consider two types of replacement parts: Part A (wood frame) and Part B (metal frame). Part A can be replaced with either another Part A or with a Part B. However, Part B can be replaced only by another Part B.

To evaluate the service level for our simulation, we aim to capture a number of operational considerations (as illustrated in Figure 3.15, left to right):

- Simulate the daily number of furniture items coming in for repair over time, and the respective required part (Part A or Part B).

- Assign the requested part, otherwise place the item into the queue and calculate service level.

- If requesting part A, check availability of part A or B and send the replaced part A for repair.

- If requesting part B, check availability of part B and send the replaced part B for repair.

- Update inventory holding to reflect outgoing parts.

Such a simulation will ascertain the ongoing service level when given the number of parts held in inventory (at some

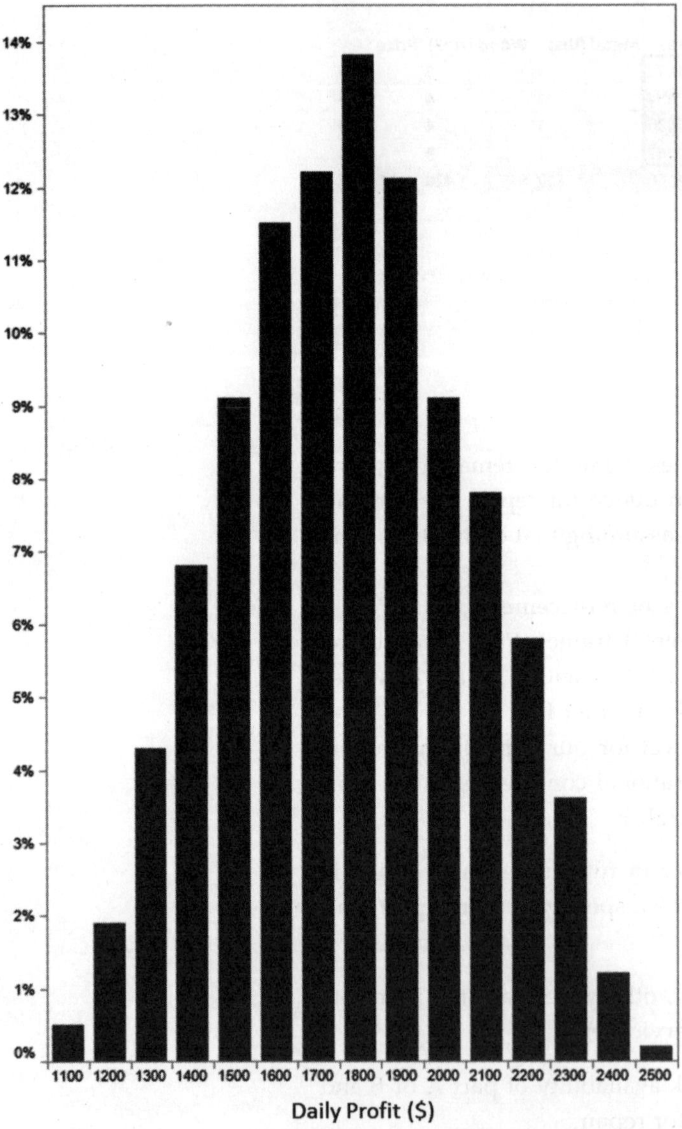

Figure 3.14: Results from 1,000 Monte Carlo runs of furniture example with randomness inserted into the labor time. The y-axis shows the percent of runs obtained for a particular profit range. The peak indicates that a profit in the range of $1,800 is most likely, but values can range between $1,100–2,500.

starting point, as the service level will change as parts are consumed and furniture is repaired), the time taken to repair each item, the service time, etc.

Figure 3.15 presents a schematic view of a recommended holistic operational solution flow. It combines forecasting, optimization and simulation in a manner that is common in practice. Given forecasts, the outcome of interest is optimized while simulating the ongoing operational variability. In this scenario, we try to capture the knowns and to quantify the unknowns. In the context of our furniture example, this means:

1. Forecast the future demand for furniture items.

2. Optimize the production mix, given constraints and forecasted demand.

3. Simulate the system given the forecasted demand, optimal holding level and domain knowledge.

Such a process will take into consideration future requirements, find the best possible configuration and simulate the solution over time.

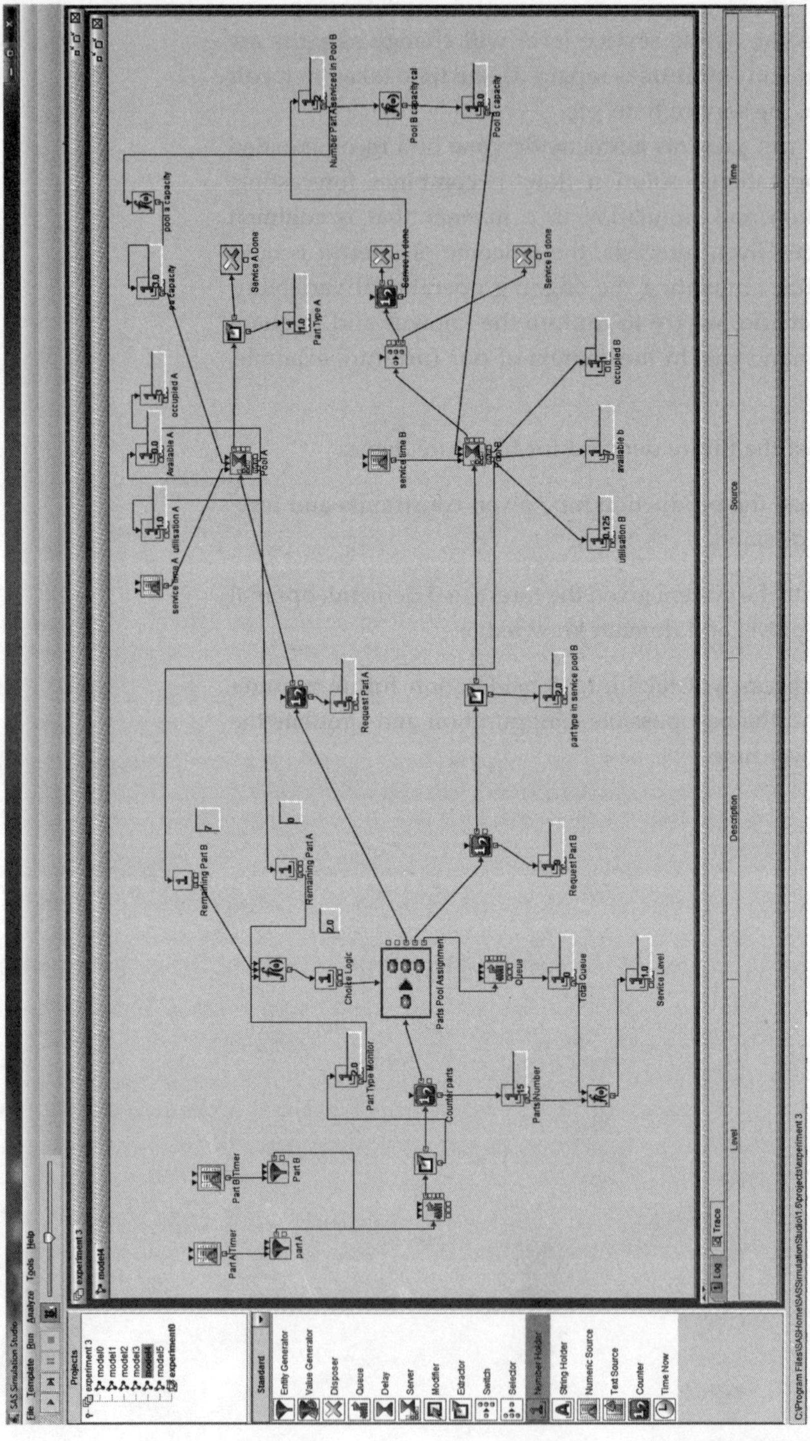

Figure 3.15: Visualization of a simulation flow of repairing furniture with two interchangeable parts.

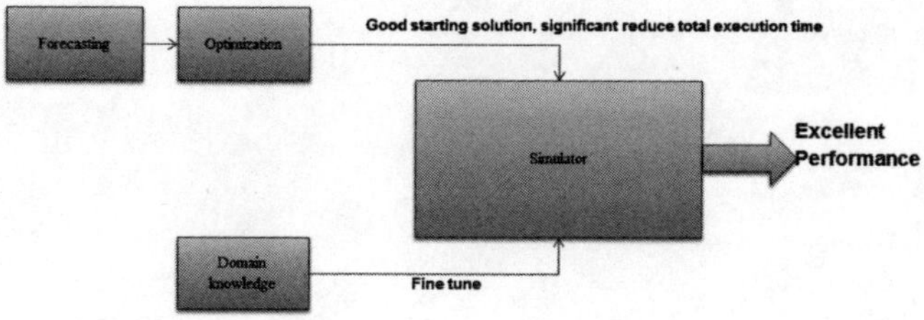

Figure 3.16: Visualisation of a holistic approach towards a complete operational system that incorporates forecasting, optimization and simulation.

4 *From Data Mining to Data Analytics*

The data mining methods and approaches described in Chapter 3 can be used in a wide range of applications and contexts. In recent years, data types and structures other than those described in the data mining chapter have become popular. Data miners took this challenge as an opportunity to expand data mining machinery in creative and useful ways.

In this chapter, we focus on two types of data structures: networks and text. We use the term *data analytics* to describe the approaches used for extracting information from network and textual data using data mining. This term implies a higher level view of the data mining tools and their integration in a more context-specific fashion.

4.1 *Network Analytics*

With the growing popularity of online social networks such as Facebook, LinkedIn, Google+, Twitter, Pinterest and many other social websites, a new type of data has emerged: social network data[1]. In addition to a set of measurements on each record, social networks give information about connectivity between records. A Facebook account is linked to all the "friends" of that account. Network data are available in many non-social contexts as well. For example, data on a mobile telephone account includes not only the account activity in terms of usage and billing, but also information on which other accounts it is linked to through calls.

[1] *The Conversation Prism* by Brian Solis and JESS3, gives you a whole view of the social media universe www.theconversationprism.com.

Network analysis, also known as *link analysis*, furthers our understanding beyond knowing what people are saying to *whom* they are saying it to. These approaches allow exploring commonalities among a group of individuals in terms of experiences such as studying at the same university during the same years, preferences such as movie or restaurant taste, social connections such as sharing a common friend, and more. The social connectivity relationships give rise to algorithms such as Facebook's and LinkedIn's "People You May Know," recommending further individuals to expand one's existing social network.

There are a number of different types of links that can be formed, based on extracted information. For instance, *hard links* are based on common attributes such as addresses and phone numbers whereas *soft links* are based on attributes with a high degree of similarity (such as a similar spelling of a name, or identical phonetics). *Transactional links* indicate involvement in the same transaction, which can also be an exchange of messages (comments or feedback on a post). *Associate links* indicate a connection to the same organization, individual or entity.

Understanding these networks allows us to determine the leaders and followers in the online world. Leaders are those whose comments and opinions are repeated among a following. These individuals are key for targeted marketing or monitoring.

In telecommunications, for instance, the person paying the family mobile bills may be more appropriate to target with new promotions, products and campaigns than the other family members. In Figure 4.1 we visualize such a link analysis to identify mobile leaders and followers.

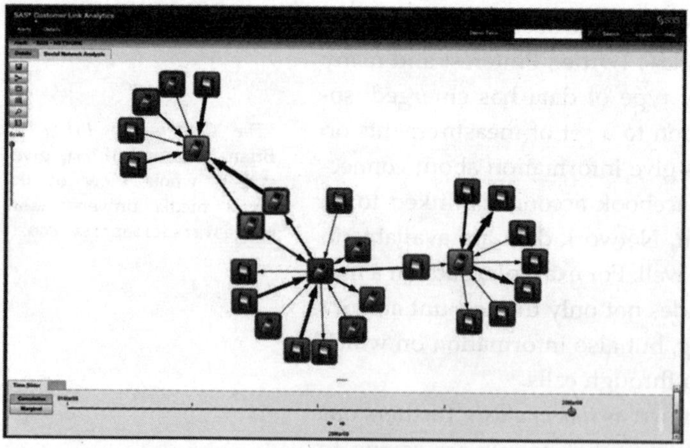

Figure 4.1: Generating and visualizing telecommunication networks allows to uncover the leaders and followers for targeted engagement and marketing.

Fraud detection is another field that benefits from link analysis. Researchers at the AT&T Lab Research group published a paper [8] on *network-based marketing*, "a collection of marketing techniques which take advantage of links between consumers to increase sales." Using a large dataset of telecom subscribers who received a promotional offer, they discovered a much higher adoption rate of the new service among those linked to a prior customer (a rate 3 to 5 times greater than baseline groups selected by the firm's marketing team). Moreover, they showed that analyzing the network data enables acquiring new customers that otherwise would not have been identified based on traditional attributes.

Network information can be utilized in various ways. One simple approach is to aggregate the user's network information into statistics such as the number of direct connections, the number of second-order connections, etc. Specific network metrics, originating in sociology, are now common in social network analysis. These metrics are measured for each node and help characterize the network structure. Four key network metrics are:

degree centrality: the number of direct connections (first-degree connections) of a user.

closeness centrality: the inverse of the sum of the shortest paths between the user and every other user in the network.

betweenness centrality: the number of shortest paths from all users to all other users that are connected to the user of interest.

eigenvector centrality: a score based on the scores of connected users (connections with high-scoring nodes contribute more to this score)

Google's PageRank measure, which ranks a web page based on the importance of web pages linking to that page (among other factors), is an example of an eigenvector centrality metric. Such statistics and metrics can then be treated as additional measurements (columns) in the ordinary dataset, and the various data mining methods applied.

A second approach is to use the connectivity information directly for inferring similarity. Networks of users help find users with similar preferences and tastes. For example, collaborative filtering or k-Nearest Neighbors can define similar users (neighbors) based on their network proximity. A marketing study [8] used telecom communication network data for identifying likely adopters for a new product. The authors show that including network information in the supervised model improves prediction accuracy.

Social Network Analysis (SNA) software ranges in capabilities. Some software packages are BI-focused and provide network visualization and possibly computation of network metrics. More BA-focused tools include data mining capabilities that integrate the network information and use it, for example, for scoring users.

A different type of network is item-based. For example, items that are purchased together are connected. An item network can highlight similar items for purposes of personalized recommendations or for deriving similarity rules. For example, in one study [2] the researchers created a product-network of books based on Amazon.com recommendations of type "Customers who purchased this item also purchased..." (see Figure 4.2). They combined the network information with book prices for the duration of a year. Using these data, the authors investigated various relationships between demand and the connectivity of books.

[2] G. Oestreicher-Singer and A. Sundararajan. The visible hand of social networks in electronic markets. *Management Science*. Published online before print, June 15, 2012.

4.2 *Text Analytics*

Text analytics is the application of data mining and other analytical methodologies to textual data for the purpose of extracting insight. The main feature of text data is that it is unstructured. In 1998, Merrill Lynch[3] estimated that approximately 80% of all usable business information exists in an unstructured representation. Hence, the need to be able to manage and extract critical business knowledge from information that [at the time could] only be handled in a laborious manual fashion. In Figure 4.3 we highlight the fundamental challenges of text data. These include the overwhelming number of data sources (social media, reports, websites, internal and external communications, etc.), issues with interpretability (different analysts interpret texts differently), and delayed response to gained insights due to the amount of time needed to process large amounts of textual data.

[3] Christopher C. Shilakes and Julie Tylman. Enterprise Information Portals. *Merrill Lynch*, November 1998.

The terms *text mining* and *text analytics* are sometimes used interchangeably. However, we distinguish between the two. Following our distinction between *data mining* (algorithms and models) and *data analytics* (the use of data mining in the context of a particular data type) we use *data analytics* as a broader term that describes the use of text data for gaining insights. We reserve *text mining* for the more technical use of data mining methods suitable for text data. In particular,

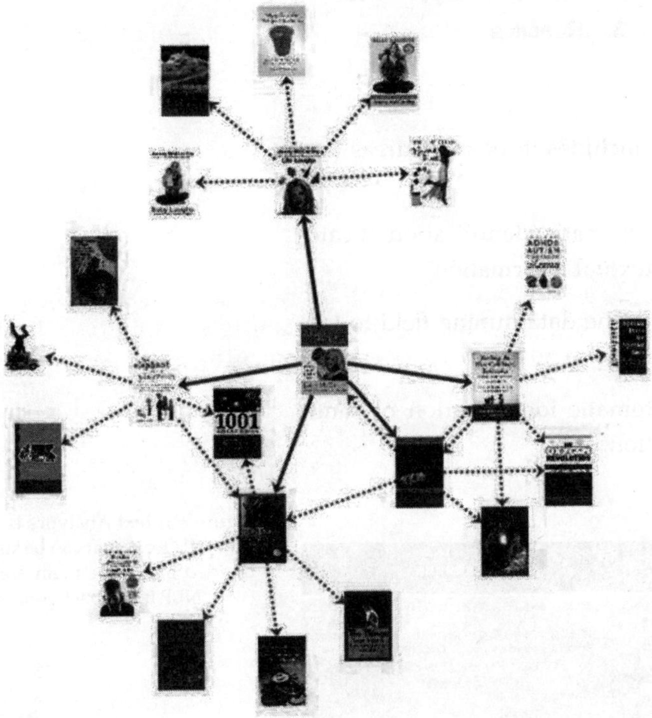

Figure 4.2: Product network for books based on Amazon.com recommendations (with permission from Gal Oestreicher-Singer and Arun Sundararajan).

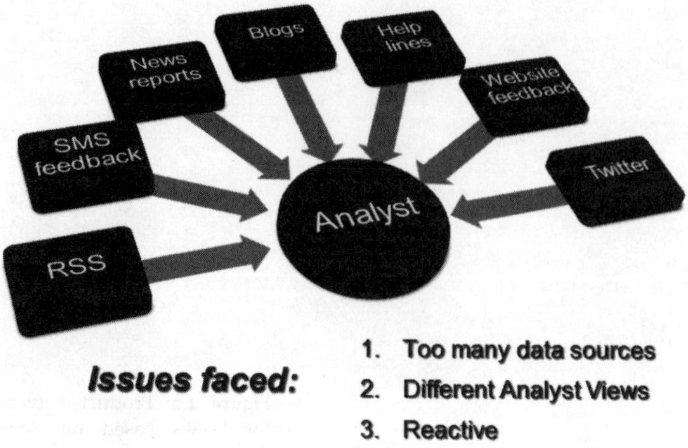

Figure 4.3: Current challenges faced by analysts when dealing with text data.

our definition of *text analytics* includes three main areas (see Figure 4.4):

- *Content Categorization:* the automatic identification of categories and concept within textual information
- *Text Mining:* the extension of the data mining field to textual information.
- *Sentiment Analysis:* the automatic identification of sentiment from textual information.

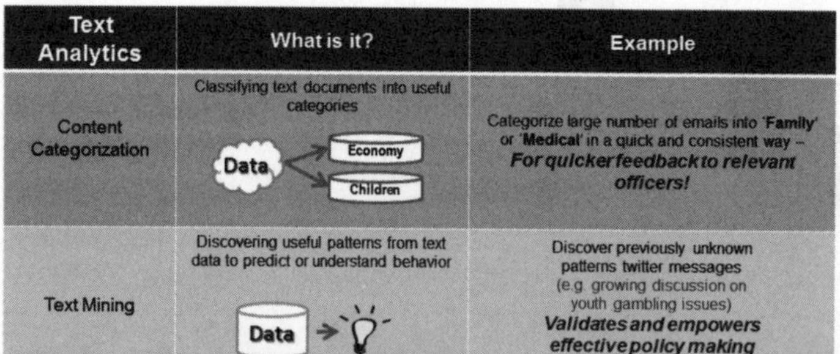

Text Analytics	What is it?	Example
Content Categorization	Classifying text documents into useful categories Data → Economy, Children	Categorize large number of emails into '**Family**' or '**Medical**' in a quick and consistent way – ***For quicker feedback to relevant officers!***
Text Mining	Discovering useful patterns from text data to predict or understand behavior Data →	Discover previously unknown patterns twitter messages (e.g. growing discussion on youth gambling issues) ***Validates and empowers effective policy making***
Sentiment Analysis	Determine if text message is positive or negative (polarity) Data → +, -	Rank feedback emails to identify top 10% most negative messages – ***Effectively prioritize issues***

Figure 4.4: Text Analytics is an umbrella term that can be subdivided into three main areas (with NLP in the background).

A recent book on text mining[4], categorized *text mining* into seven practice areas:

[4] G. Miner, Dursun Delen, J. Elder, A. Fast, T. Hill, and R. A. Nisbet. *Practical Text Mining and Statistical Analysis for Non-Structured Text Data Applications*. Academic Press, Waltham, Mass., 2012.

1. *Search and information retrieval* – finding documents that match search keywords
2. *Document clustering* – unsupervised clustering based on similar search criteria
3. *Document classification* – supervised classification based on the text in a document
4. *Web mining* – classifying and modeling structured Web data
5. *Information extraction* – converting unstructured text data to structured data
6. *Natural Language Processing* – finding grammatical cues and phrase boundaries
7. *Concept extraction* – determining meaning within context (combining human and machine intelligence).

This list includes practice areas that rely on computer and database algorithms such as search algorithms, on data mining methods such as supervised and unsupervised learning methods, on human domain expertise, and on combinations of the above. We focus in particular on Natural Language Processing (NLP), a background capability used within and throughout each of the three text analytics areas we listed earlier.

Natural Language Processing (NLP)

It is impossible to discuss text analytics without referring to Natural Language Processing (NLP). One of the most challenging aspects of text-based information is language, not just the occurrence of words that generate meaning but the contextual information of how they appear. This notion dates back to 1950, with Alan Turing's famous Turing Test as the criterion for intelligence[5]. The test is whether a computer can imitate a human in real-time conversation so that the human is unable to detect whether the counterpart is human or machine.

[5] en.wikipedia.org/wiki/Computing_Machinery_and_Intelligence.

The field of NLP (computational linguistifcs), studies human language from a computational perspective, and develops algorithms and mathematical models for processing natural language, such as sound and speech. Earlier, NLP involved the direct hand coding of large sets of rules. Today, modern NLP algorithms are based on machine learning and on some domain knowledge. NLP technologies are used for parsing (separating) sentences into words and other components and for characterizing these components in terms of their roles. This task is often context-dependent and obviously language-dependent. For example, some written languages do not have spaces between words. Another step consists of removing stop-words such as "a, the, etc.". An important NLP operation is trimming words ("stemming") to their root form. For example, "purchasing" and "purchased" would be stemmed to "purchase".

NLP is used in many popular applications such as machine translation. For example, Google Translate[6] uses computer algorithms to learn from human-translated text[7]:

> By detecting patterns in documents that have already been translated by human translators, Google Translate can make intelligent guesses as to what an appropriate translation should be. This process of seeking patterns in large amounts of text is called "statistical machine translation." Since the translations are generated by machines, not all translation will be perfect.

[6] `translate.google.com`.

[7] `translate.google.com/about`.

Figure 4.5: Machine translation is one example of NLP applications.

Another example of an online NLP application is Accentuate.us, a free, open-source add-on to the Firefox browser. This add-on simplifies and speeds up typing in languages that use Latin with special characters (such as Vietnamese, French, and many African languages). Users type text in plain ASCII, and the application automatically adds all diacritics and special characters in the correct places. The tool is also useful when an ordinary keyboard is available. How does Accentuate.us work? From the Accentuate.us website:

> Accentuate.us uses statistics to predict where special characters are needed on a language-by-language basis

More detail is available in a blog post by the creators of the application[8]:

> Accentuate.us uses a machine learning approach, employing both character-level and word-level models trained on data crawled from the web for more than 100 languages.

[8] `www.dataists.com/category/machine-learning-in-the-real-world`; technical paper available at `borel.slu.edu/pub/lre.pdf`

And to drill down even further, the application uses a machine learning algorithm that is based on *unicodification*, which is "a mapping from a subset of all Unicode characters into (strings of zero or more) ASCII characters (Unicode 0000-007F)." It also relies on open-source spell checking dictionaries.

NLP is widely used behind the scenes of text analytics as the engine that breaks down text into meaningful bits of information or semantically meaningful content [9]. We will discuss its role in each of the three text analytics areas next.

[9] S. Hill, F. Provost, and Volinsky C. Models of natural language understanding. In *Proceedings of the National Academy of Sciences of the United States of America*, volume 92, pages 9977–9982, 1995; Steven Bird, Ewan Klein, and Edward Loper. *Natural Language Processing with Python*. O'Reilly Media, 2009; and Daniel Jurafsky and James H. Martin. *Speech and Language Processing, 2nd edition*. Pearson Prentice Hall, 2008.

Content Categorization

The focus of the first area of text analytics, content categorization, is about identifying what "you already know." Context categorization is therefore part of information management rather than a business analytics technique. However, content categorization is an important step in the text analytics process: it helps automate and speed up the manual process of categorizing documents in which hundreds of man-hours are regularly invested in reading texts and identifying keywords and contextual information. Instead, content categorization algorithms can automate and streamline the process of reviewing and tagging textual information.

Given that content categorization is about capturing known information, the first step is creating a taxonomy, a list of relevant words and phrases that encapsulates the information we are searching for. Such taxonomies can include simple representations of the words to be identified, or using NLP, a more elaborate representation of relevant terms (verbs, nouns, relationship between terms, etc.). Figure 4.6 illustrates a taxonomy related to housing information that might be used by a real-estate agency to categorize documents. Figure 4.7 shows the application of this taxonomy to a document. We can see the terms of interest highlighted in the document, which can then be used for categorizing the document (for future searches). The layer of content categorization would subsequently feed into a layer of analysis, modeling and reporting.

SRA, a US government provider of technology and consulting, used the approach of content categorization[10] to re-index a library collection of hundreds of thousands of reports from over 100 years. The process was completed in only hours, rather than months or years. In terms of coverage, SRA was able to categorize the documents 90% of the time in comparison to 75% coverage achieved by human indexers.

[10] Copyright ©SAS Institute Inc. Cary, NC, USA `www.sas.com/success/sra.html`.

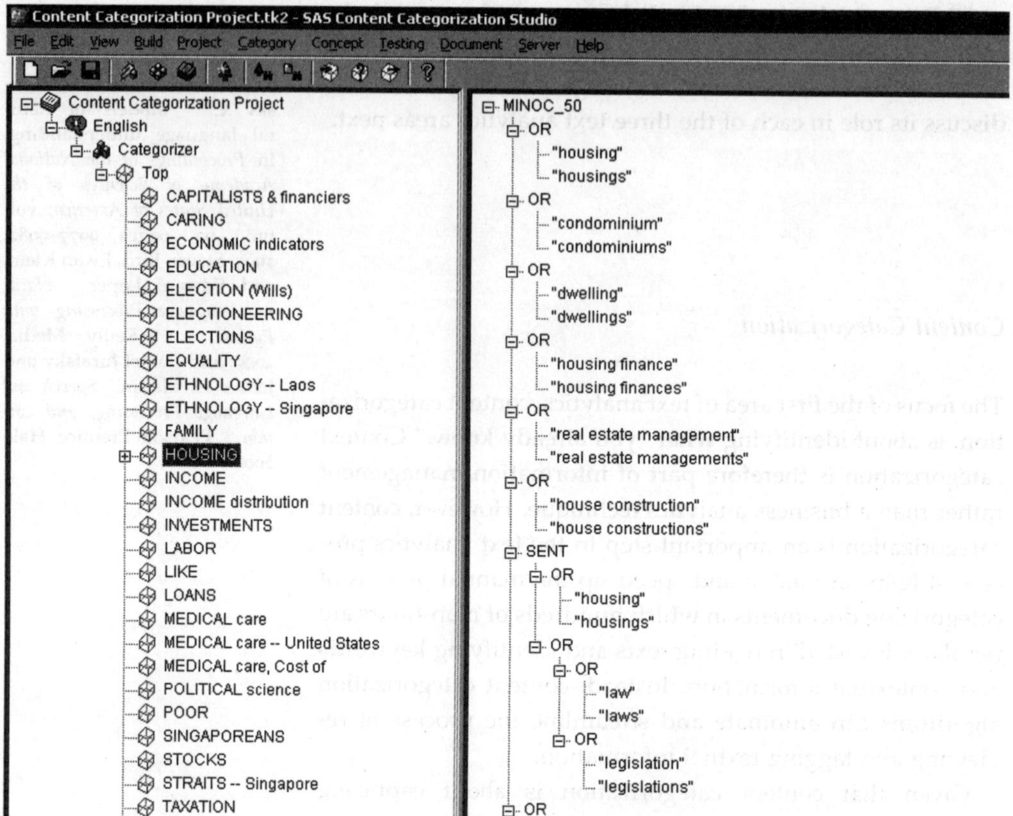

Figure 4.6: An example of a taxonomy relating to Housing information.

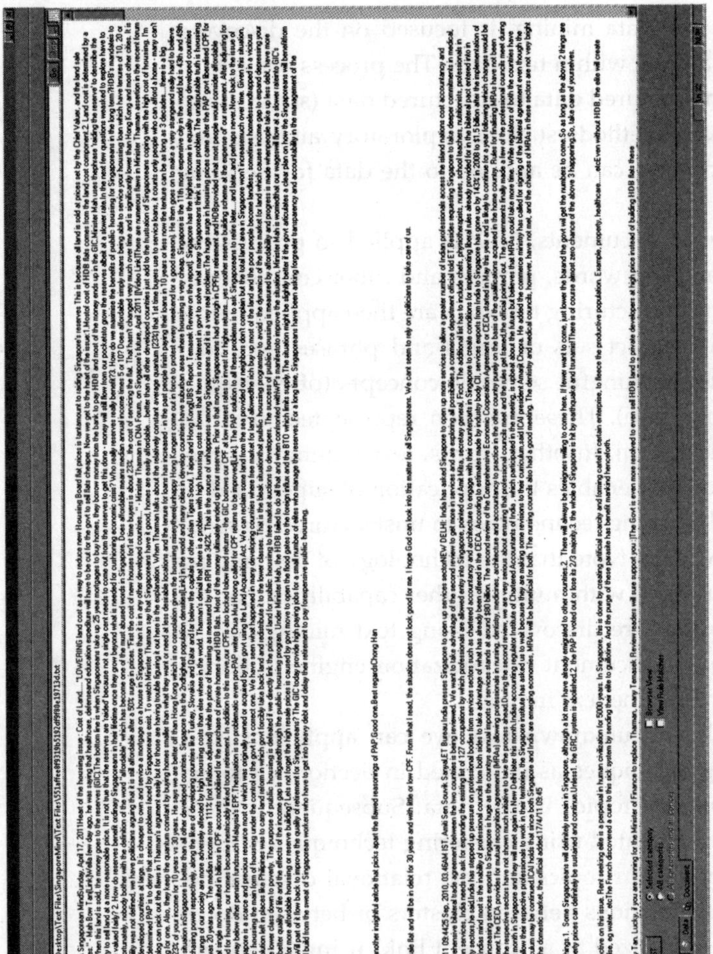

Figure 4.7: Automatically identifying and indexing a document containing instances referring to "housing" and "public housing" for easy document categorization and searching.

Text Mining

Text mining, like data mining, is focused on the discovery of *unknown* patterns within text data. The process consists of converting unstructured data to structured data (structuring) so that ordinary methods such as exploratory analysis and predictive modeling can be applied to the data for deriving insight.

Given a set of documents, NLP is applied to process the information and tag words, phrases and other components. Technologies for structuring text data are then applied to this information to extract sets of terms and phrases and convert them into meaningful semantic concepts (often requiring human expertise). These are then represented in structured numerical form. In other words, text mining is a preprocessing step that enables the application of supervised or unsupervised learning technologies to unstructured or semi-structured text data. Note that the technology of text mining works hand-in-hand with multiple other capabilities. For example, topics that are discovered using text mining can be fed back into the document categorization engine to enrich and operationalize the text mining.

When analyzing unknown text, we can apply unsupervised learning techniques as illustrated in Section 3.2 to extract and represent topics in the data. Subsequently, these topics can be segmented using clustering techniques to identify clusters of similar topics and the relational distance between clusters. Relations between clusters or between documents can be visualized as a "concept link" using a network chart. Repeating this analysis over time and monitoring the network chart can help reveal emerging trends or dramatic changes. An example is shown in Figure 4.8, where words are clustered using hierarchical clustering. While this example illustrates the use of clustering, it is important to note that all the data mining capabilities and methodologies that can be applied to structured numerical data are also applicable to text data, after structuring it using text mining.

Text mining is becoming popular among insurance companies for revealing suspect claims. Insurance companies typically have many sources of textual data, from underwriting notes and diaries to reports based on customer interactions. An example is AFA Insurance[11] that regularly applies text mining to insurance claims to identify potentially fraudulent claims. In a different context, The Hong Kong Ef-

[11] Copyright ©SAS Institute Inc. Cary, NC, USA `www.sas.com/success/afa.html`.

ficiency Unit[12] applies text mining to citizens' complaints to identify (potentially hidden) root-causes to focus on and remedy. Rather than reviewing each of the complaint documents manually, the objective is to automatically identify insight that can be quickly acted upon.

[12] Copyright ©SAS Institute Inc. Cary, NC, USA `www.sas.com/success/hongkongeu.html`.

Sentiment Analysis

Sentiment analysis is one of the more popular applications in text analytics, focusing on automatic inferences of human sentiment directly from text. By "sentiment" we refer to a wide range of emotions, from negative to positive.

The technology behind sentiment analysis combines three "engines":

1. NLP – handles concept and semantic representation of language
2. Terms dictionary – captures domain expertise with regard to negativity and positivity
3. Statistical engine – automatically identifies new terms that are used in a negative or positive context.

Figure 4.10 illustrates a sentiment analysis model that combines NLP rules with a terms dictionary.

Figure 4.11 illustrates an example of applying a sentiment engine to text. Color is used to represent the positiveness or negativeness of each term (the color figure is available on the book companion website).

It is important to distinguish between words that have a semantic meaning of being positive or negative, such as "good," "bad," "happy," or "irritate," and words that result in the entire document[13] having a positive or negative sentiment. Words that have a positive or negative meaning are usually captured in the *terms dictionary* where we dictate, in advance, what we already know (or believe we know). However, words resulting in a document having positive or negative meaning are learned automatically through the statistical engine (what we don't know we don't know). Note that these words may not, in themselves, have any positive or negative meaning.

[13] We refer to a document being any collection of text such as: comment, post, blog, tweet, etc.

The necessity for the flexibility to learn sentiment is due to how language is used. In many cases, negative documents are written with positive language, and less frequently, positive documents written with negative language. Thus, the

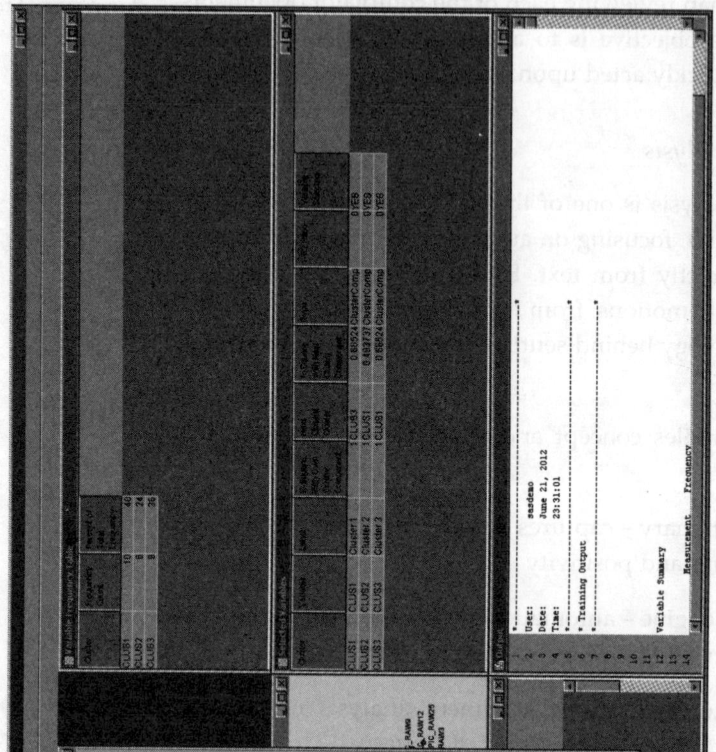

Figure 4.8: In text mining, clustering techniques can be applied to text.

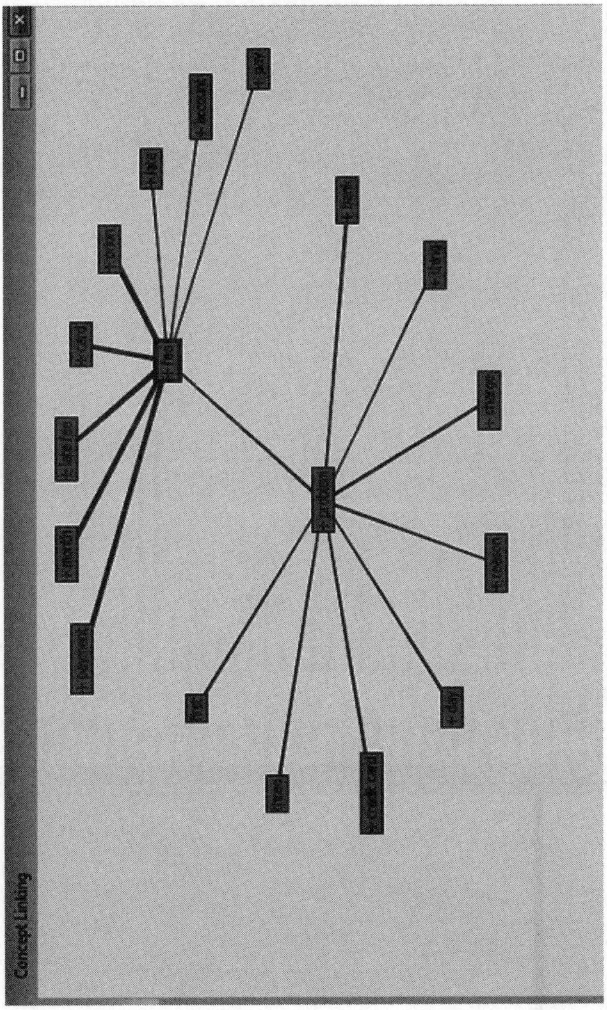

Figure 4.9: The clusters computed in Figure 4.8 can then be analyzed through link analysis to identify emerging trends or to monitor changes.

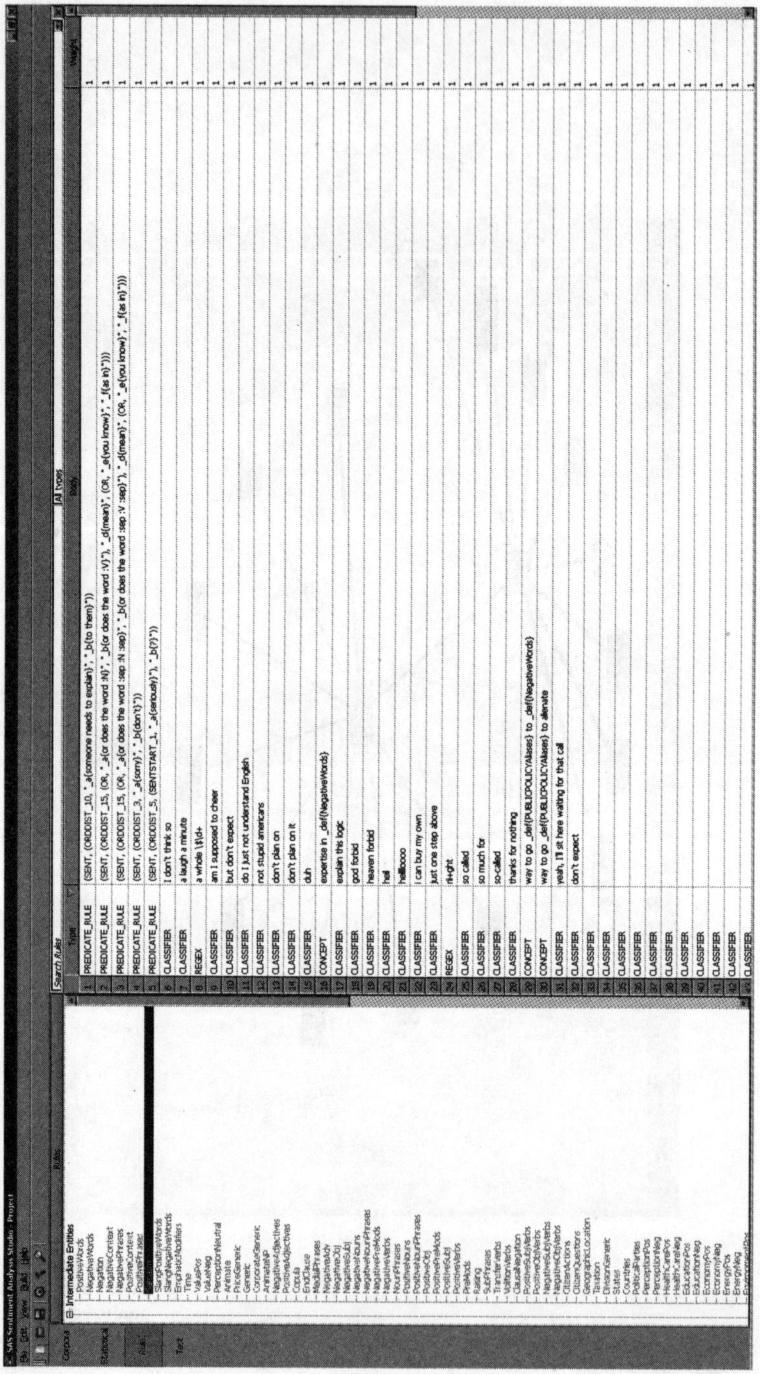

Figure 4.10: Example of a sentiment model that combines NLP rules (concepts and regular expressions) with a terms dictionary.

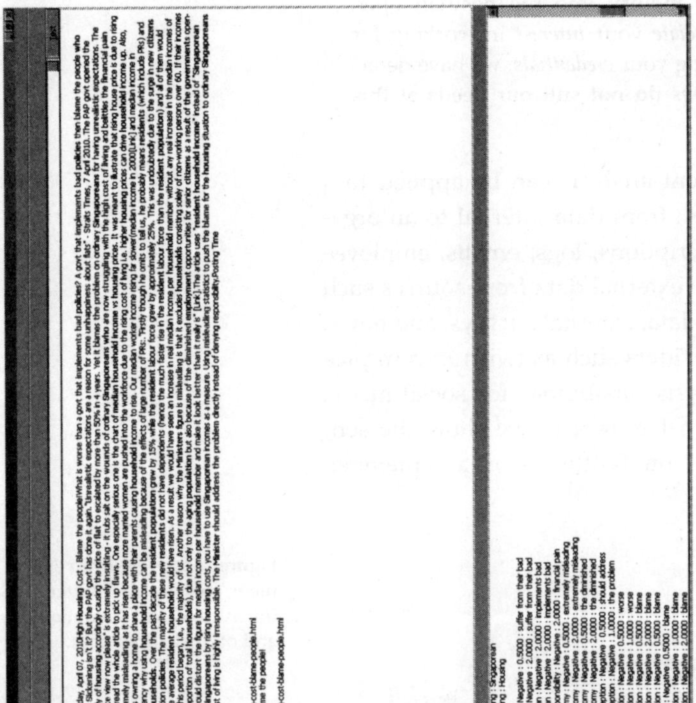

Figure 4.11: Example of applying the sentiment engine on data. Highlighted words are indicative of positive and negative terms. A color version of this figure (available on the book companion website) shows the positive terms are in Green, negative terms are in Red and categories (topics) are in Blue.

meaning of the individual words is insufficient for determining the overall sentiment. As a simple example, consider the following rejection letter:

> *Thank you* for your recent inquiry into the position open at ABC. We certainly *appreciate* your *interest* in working for our business. After reviewing your *credentials*, we have determined that your *qualifications* **do not** suit our needs at this time.

In organizations, sentiment analysis can be applied to a wide variety of data sources, from data internal to an organization, such as call transcriptions, logs, emails, employee reviews, internal surveys, to external data from sources such as social media, third party data, external surveys, and news.

Today, online service providers such as twitrratr.com provide online sentiment analysis capabilities for social media data, in this case Twitter. In Figure 4.12 we show the sentiments towards "Analytics" on Twitter as on 2 September, 2012.

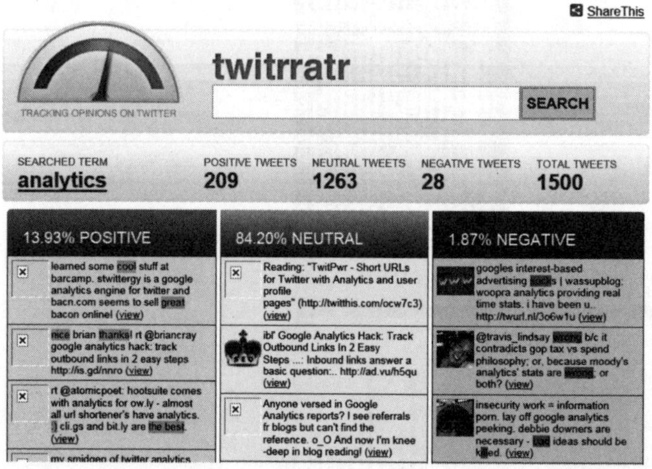

Figure 4.12: Twitrratr sentiment analysis of Twitter sentiment toward "Analytics" on 2nd of September 2012.

Another interesting recent application of sentiment analysis to Twitter data is provided through a dashboard by TIBCO and Attivio, showing live information about Twitter user sentiment for athletes and keywords in the 2012 London Olympics[14]. Figure 4.13 shows a screenshot of this application, showing Twitter sentiment for Michael Phelps over time.

[14] spotfire.tibco.com/demos/london-athletes.aspx

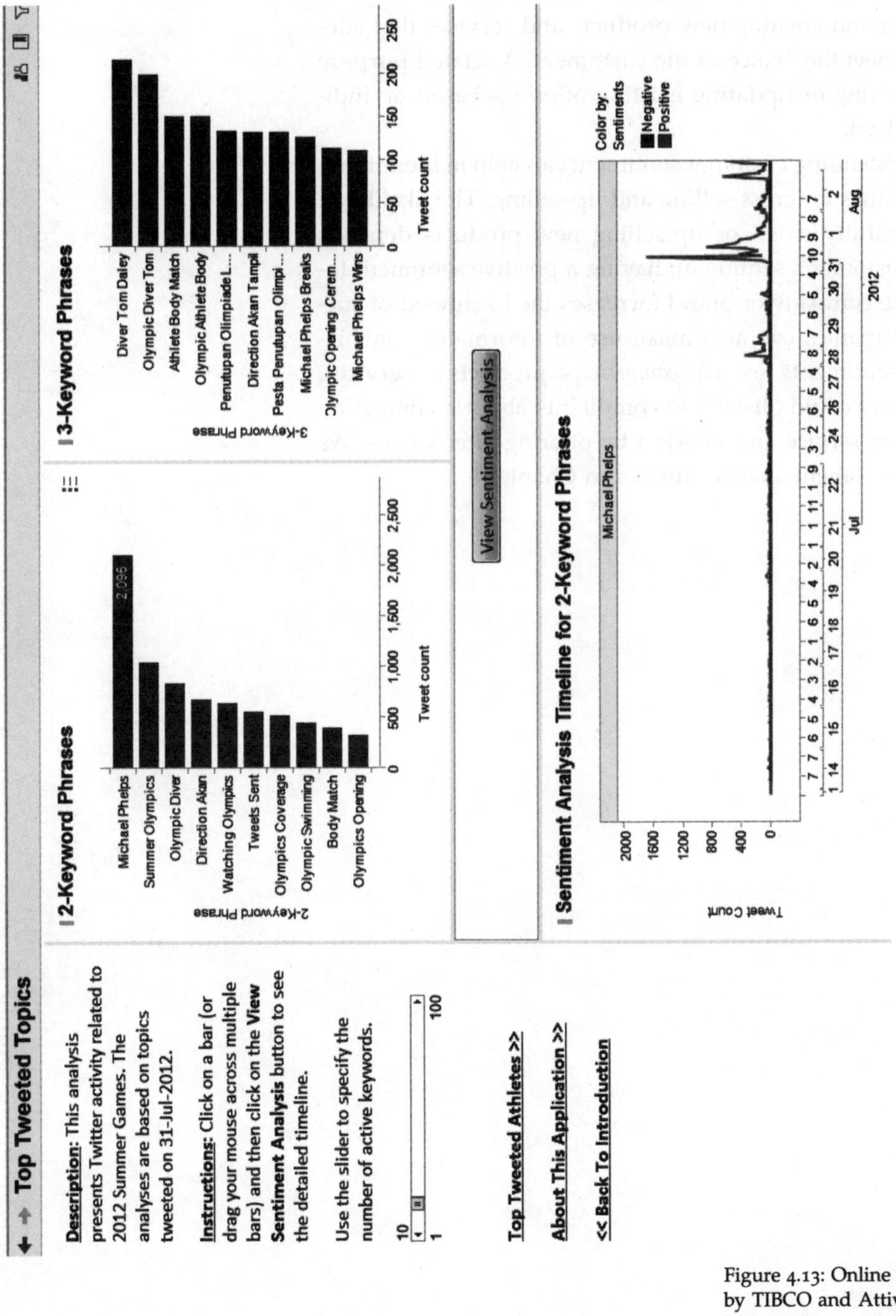

Figure 4.13: Online dashboard by TIBCO and Attivio that allows users to explore sentiment on Twitter toward different athletes in the 2012 London Olympic games.

The most common motivation for using sentiment analysis in business is to better understand customers. One purpose is to be able to better align existing products and services with customers' needs and desires. Another purpose is in designing and creating new products and services that adequately meet the "voice of the customer." A related purpose is for revising or updating existing offerings based on indirect feedback.

Understanding customer sentiment can help in identifying opportunities for cross-selling and up-selling. The likelihood of successfully cross- or up-selling new products depends on the customer's sentiment; having a positive sentiment towards the company or brand increases the likelihood of success. Companies can also make use of information on customers' sentiments towards *competitors'* products or services. A company could "listen" to complaints about a competing product or service and interject by offering alternatives. We discuss sentiment analysis further in Chapter 6.

Part III

Business Analytics

5 *Customer Analytics*

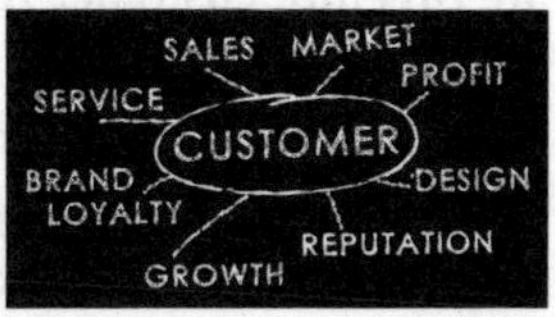

In the past, limited choices of products and services created a corporate attitude of "if we sell, they will buy." Companies diverted resources to provide preferential treatment to their VIP clientele, while ignoring needs of the general customer base.

In hindsight, this approach was logical from a business point of view, because the expenses associated with preferential treatment were higher than the loss of a handful of non-VIP customers. However, with the ever-increasing number of service providers and products, and with the growing ease that customers can switch between providers, it has become crucial for companies to invest in customer acquisition and retention beyond that of the VIP clientele.

YOUR BRAND IS CREATED OUT OF CUSTOMER CONTACT AND THE EXPERIENCE YOUR CUSTOMERS HAVE OF YOU.

— Stelios Haji–Ioannou (1967–)
Chairman, EasyGroup

Companies today use different approaches to understand the needs and desires of existing and potential customers, in order to retain customer loyalty and to increase wallet share. Market research, and in particular the study of customer preferences, has evolved with technology from obtrusive face-to-face and phone interviews and focus groups, to less obtrusive Internet and email surveys, and now to unobtrusive analysis of online behavior via click-stream data, online purchase data, social media postings, and more.

Interestingly, the challenge posed by competition is not only outward facing, in terms of competing with similar product providers, but inward as well. Within a company, different departments compete for the same customers to offer competing services. For example, a bank offers various products such as personal loans, credit cards, and mortgages through different channels, thereby affecting not only potential customers but also existing clientele. The reality of organizations is that there are multiple products that can be offered through multiple channels with different services, offers and pricing.

How do we know which products or services to offer existing customers to match their individual needs? How do we preempt customer requirements and desires without explicit interaction? Knowing one's customers is imperative to improving customer satisfaction, choosing better directions for company growth, and gaining a competitive advantage.

The customer analytics approach can range from in-depth analytics based on a small number of customers to analytics aimed at a global understanding of a mass consumer population. Companies and organizations range, in terms of the types of customers that they concentrate on, from focusing on small, niche groups of clients to catering to a mass segment of the population (Figure 5.1).

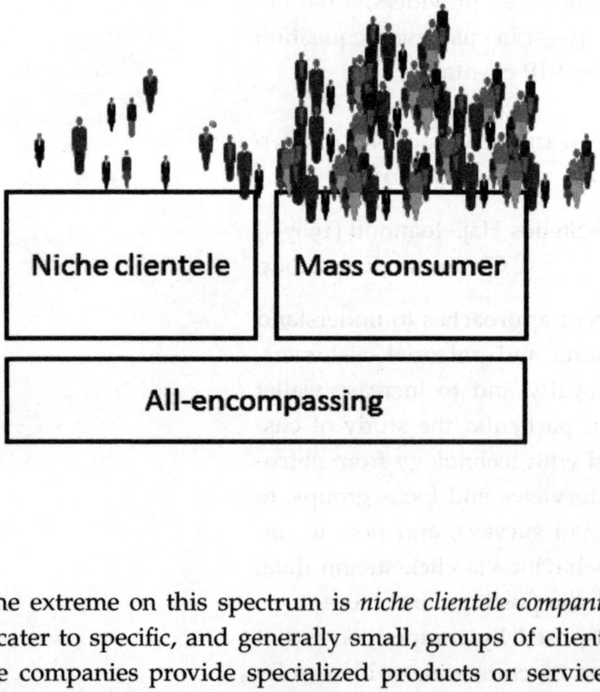

Figure 5.1: Companies and organizations range from focusing on small, niche groups of clients, catering to a mass segment of the population and companies that cater to both niche clientele and mass consumers.

One extreme on this spectrum is *niche clientele companies* that cater to specific, and generally small, groups of clients. These companies provide specialized products or services. Examples include high-value sports car manufacturers such as Lamborghini and Bugatti and the matchmaking service *Seventy Thirty*, which requires that both male and female members have assets worth £1m and which charges yearly fees of £10,000. Other, less wealth-focused companies include organic supermarkets, adult shops and art film houses.

The other extreme is *mass consumer companies*, which typically offer services or products of interest to a large population. A main example is "no frills" companies, which offer products or services for which the non-essential features have been removed to keep the price low. In these cases, "non-essential" refers to anything but the bare-basic level required. "No frills" companies include airlines such as Southwest, easyJet, Ryanair[1], Tiger Airways and Air Asia; retailers such as Argos and Primark in the UK and Walmart in the USA; and many mobile phone service providers.

[1] Ryanair has even gone to the extreme of considering aircraft lavatory charges (`www.guardian.co.uk/business/2009/mar/05/ryanair-toilet-charge/`, accessed Oct 2011).

In between the two extremes lie *all-encompassing companies* that cater to both niche clientele and mass consumer audiences. Examples include private banking, supermarkets, major airlines, cable and TV companies, and many retailers. "Freemium" services such as Skype and LinkedIn are also all-encompassing. Using the basic features is free, but extra services require payment. These companies, while focusing on the general public, often have special schemes and rewards for high spenders, frequent patrons and high net-worth individuals. Such companies also typically have a larger range of product offerings to accommodate different audiences.

Customer analytics (know-thy-customer and targeted marketing) is essential to achieving business objectives in companies, no matter their position on the customer type spectrum. The type of customer analytics, however, manifests itself in different ways. The underlying commonality is increasing company value with existing customers. In most cases, value is monetary, whether the organization is a commercial enterprise or a socially-oriented non-for-profit organization.

Customer analytics is highly valuable not only for commercial companies, but also for non-for-profit organizations, NGOs, and social-focused companies, since they too must deliver value to their customers while remaining financially solvent. Blood banks and kidney registries are "niche clientele organizations" that must know their clients, both donors and recipients, sufficiently well in order to offer valuable and safe services. Organizations such as the American Red Cross and World Vision International can be considered all-encompassing organizations in terms of their donors. In addition to the general public and anonymous donors, frequent donors typically donate large amounts of money.

Finally, micro-financing organizations such as Grameen Bank[2] are examples of mass consumer organizations in that they provide small loans to large numbers of customers with similar backgrounds.

[2] Grameen Bank (GB) has reversed conventional banking practice by removing the need for collateral and created a banking system based on mutual trust, accountability, participation and creativity. GB provides credit to the poorest of the poor in rural Bangladesh, without any collateral www.grameen.com.

Let us first describe the types of data that companies can collect on customers and then consider the types of business analytics goals and data mining techniques that are useful for gaining knowledge from the data.

Customer Data

Thanks to recent advances in information technologies, the collection, transfer, and storage of large amounts of data has now become cheaper and faster[3]. Companies and organizations now routinely collect and maintain customer databases to create a "360° view" of their customers in the hope that the data can be used for some useful purpose in the future.

[3] See also reference to High Performance Analytics in Chapter 1.

Data are automatically collected on many aspects of each transaction that takes place. Transaction information includes details about the transaction itself (what was purchased, how many items, what price was paid, whether a coupon was used, etc.) as well as meta-data (time of transaction, store number, cashier name, etc.).

Data may also be available at the customer level, when customers are identifiable. One example is via loyalty cards, where customers identify themselves by presenting their loyalty card at checkout. Another example is eCommerce, where users are required to create an account linked to their email address. Customer identity (in some form) can be linked to the transactional data when customer details are required for a transaction to go through, such as credit card or PayPal transactions, bank loans and car rentals.

In India, Aadhar[4] is a newly launched program on a massive scale, aimed at providing every citizen with a unique identification number. In addition to usage for governmental transactions, such as receiving social security funds, the ID is also intended for use in a wide range of commercial applications, such as loans from micro-financing organizations. Several countries have already implemented similar initiatives; Singapore introduced the concept of a national registration identity card in 1965[5].

[4] uidai.gov.in/aadhaar.html.

[5] www.ica.gov.sg/services_centre_overview.aspx?pageid=264.

Transactional data, especially in eCommerce, may also include click-stream data that show the customer trail from the moment of entry to the store or website, until exit, whether a transaction was completed or not. Examining click-stream data can provide insight regarding web usability and also flag potential problems. It can be used, taking a machine learning approach, to learn about individual customer behavior, thereby increasing "know-thy-customers."

In addition to transactional data passively collected, companies may actively pursue further customer information by including mandatory or optional personal questions on a sign-up form for a loyalty card, or when opening an account. Data may be actively collected about customer feedback, using technologies ranging from solicited customer surveys to collecting unsolicited feedback from social media.

The amount of effort involved in such active data collection depends on its perceived usefulness to the company, given collection costs. For example, the travel website Expedia[6] effectively uses analytics to combine customer data with click-stream information to

> *understand what marketing promotional channels influence and drive revenue conversions on the site; optimize its marketing spend by channel; increase customer lifetime value; and improve the overall experience of customers while on the site. The latter recently helped the company avoid millions of dollars in reservation losses.*

[6] Copyright ©SAS Institute Inc. Cary, NC, USA `www.sas.com/success/expedia_travel.html`.

The quantity and type of customer information needed in addition to transactional data depends on the customer-type spectrum discussed earlier.

In niche clientele companies, highly detailed data is collected on a small number of customers. The main business analytics challenge is the small sample size. However, the richness of the data results from the wealth of information on each customer, which includes historical information from different sources. This data richness enables the prediction of future requirements and actions of special customers.

Timeliness is another important feature of customer data. Timely data can be used for choosing effective marketing engagements. An essential element of mass consumer marketing is quick learning and reaction. Failed product offerings must be identified as soon as possible due to lack of customer loyalty.

Customer data may also change over time: demographic information such as marital status, income level and number of children, geographic location, transaction behavior, and more. Collecting and maintaining up-to-date information can prove highly useful. A somewhat extreme example of using change in customers' behavioral data is the giant retailer Target, who made headlines in 2012 for its ability to identify when shoppers were pregnant. They did this by using analytics to identify changes in shopping habits at early stages of pregnancy[7].

[7] www.dailymail.co.uk/news/article-2102859/.

Although mass consumer companies may not be interested in pro-actively collecting individual customer-level data due to their interest in overall behavior, such data are often automatically available: no-frills airlines can easily obtain data on where a customer flies, how they booked the ticket, how much they paid, and additional services purchased. Low-cost insurance companies such as Geico have information on potential customers who filled out an online quote request, as well as a wealth of information on existing customers and their claims. These data can become very useful, especially when companies start expanding their offerings, thereby entering the all-encompassing arena.

5.1 *"Know Thy Customer"*

THE FIRST STEP IN EXCEEDING YOUR CUSTOMER'S EXPECTATIONS IS TO KNOW THOSE EXPECTATIONS.

— Roy H. Williams (1958–)
Author and Marketing Consultant

"Know thy customer" refers to usage of all customer data to better understand customer behavior. When considering the spectrum of focus, the required knowledge (depth and breadth) differs from niche clientele to mass customer audiences.

Niche clientele companies must know their potential and existing customers, even to the extent of following them on social media platforms such as Twitter and Facebook, understanding their comments, mood swings, and their changing preferences. Such information allows the company to provide relevant services and products tailored to the individual based on their behavioral characteristics. For example, a luxury hotel chain may follow the social media posts of a VIP as she travels around the globe, to better understand her preferences (likes and dislikes) of restaurants, entertainment, and related services.

Mass consumer companies target en masse without any personalization. Customers of low-cost companies are extremely price sensitive and are driven entirely by getting the lowest price. Their loyalty is limited, and they do not hesitate to switch to a competitor. Despite the lack of personalization and the lack of customer loyalty, it is still important to be able to *understand the customer base*, their choices, feedback, and mode of engagement with the organization. For example, no-frills airlines must figure out *where* the masses want to fly, *when* they are likely to fly, and *why* they fly.

No-frills retailers need to know *what* products their customers require or want to purchase, *how much* they will be purchasing, *when* they are likely to purchase which products, and *at what price*. Micro-financing agencies must know *how much* a typical loan is, *what terms* loan requesters will adhere to, and *what type* of loans are sought. Such information is required for understanding what products are more likely to succeed with mass consumers.

All-encompassing companies need to have the flexibility to cater to a wide range of clientele, from an in-depth understanding of individual high-value clients to an overall understanding of the mass consumer audience. Customer analytics is used in the two ways described above by both niche clientele and mass consumer companies. In addition, all-encompassing organizations have an added objective of wanting to transform the run-of-the-mill customer into a loyal or even a niche customer.

In all-encompassing companies, customer analytics is also used to figure out *how*, *why*, and *when* a mass consumer will become more loyal or even turn into a niche customer. The level of personalized data and communication with mass consumers in all-encompassing companies is not as in-depth as that for niche clientele; it is, however, significantly higher than the mass consumer level. Customer analytics is used to identify and prompt relevant products and relevant communication channels to individuals, to increase their loyalty.

Customer analytics is also used for determining the best timing to offer a new product. For instance, it would not be wise to call a customer and offer a new loan or credit card if they had just recently called to complain. Similarly, customer analytics are used to determine the tipping point that motivates customers to upgrade their relationship with the company. What factors influence stadium or theater visitors to purchase more expensive seats: price, group size, type of game/show, timing, a combination etc? Is it the price? The game/show? The size of group? A combination of these? Analytical techniques can be used to try to predict such behavior, to subsequently drive better targeted business actions.

Telstra Coporation recently demonstrated the use of analytics to both pre-empt customer complaints and improve service by identifying the root causes that led to customer complaints in a specified timeframe [8,9]. Data on customer demographics, products and billing data, customer interaction data, service orders, requests, faults and payment history was combined to build a prediction model to identify which customers will lodge a complaint.

[8] Estelle Marianne, Nick Merry, and Wendy Au. Customer experience modeling. In *SAS Global Forum 2012*, number 107-2012, 2012.

[9] `support.sas.com/resources/papers/proceedings12/107-2012.pdf`.

Relevant Data Mining Techniques

The choice of data mining methods is closely dependent on the required level of personalization. Niche clientele applications require high levels of personalization to understand what customers want and when. The mass consumer context calls for methods that uncover overall trends and aggregate behavior. All-encompassing companies employ a combination of both levels and hence a wider range of methods.

One business analytics approach to "knowing thy customer" is segmenting customers into different behavioral groups and profiling each of these groups in terms of their preferences, lifestyles and purchase behaviors. Data mining methods are then used to uncover and gain insight into the behaviors, actions and preferences of different segments.

Current standard practices segment customers using various demographic attributes, such as age, gender, geography and income. Each of these attributes is then linked to different behavioral patterns by exploring a possible relationship between a particular attribute and certain behavioral patterns. Such relationship analysis is known as *univariate analysis*. For example: what is the age group of readers who borrow *Dungeons & Dragons* books from the library? What is their gender? While such standard customer profiling and segmentation approaches are useful, they lack a wider holistic perspective of the behavior we want to capture.

First, these analyses are performed manually, or quasi-manually, using a small number of attributes. Second, each attribute is analysed separately and pre-identified. In other words, we already know the attributes for which we want to explore a relationship with an outcome of interest. Behavioral patterns are usually too complex to capture in this simplistic fashion. To be able to capture a certain behavioral aspect, one needs to simultaneously look at multiple attributes, and to consider as many attributes as possible. This type of analysis is called *multivariate analysis*. In this type of problem, we do not know what the resulting profile or segment will look like, only that it will differ from other segments in terms of the behavior of interest.

The market research company Claritas Inc., which was acquired by The Nielsen Company, created several market segmentation schemes aimed at helping companies answer these four questions:

1. Who are my potential customers?
2. What are they like?
3. Where can I find them?
4. How can I reach them?

These schemes were created in the 1990s and are still in wide use today. The segmentation is based on demographic, geographic and purchase data of households in the USA. For example, lifestyle segmentation identifies household segments such as "movers and shakers," "money and brains," and "bohemian mix." Their segmentation based on social information, further groups the lifestyle segments by affluence and urbanization levels[10].

[10] see `www.claritas.com/MyBestSegments/Default.jsp` for further details about Claritas-Nielsen's market segmentation.

Data mining techniques allow us to uncover insights in an unsupervised fashion; we do not know what type of groupings we are looking for in advance. The challenge of customer segmentation is therefore a perfect candidate for unsupervised methods (see Chapter 3). The most natural and common segmentation technique in business analytics is *Clustering* . Clustering is an automated way for creating customer segments that differ in terms of behavioral profiles. Clustering is applied to the information in the companies' customer database, which includes information such as customer-specific demographic data, personal information, purchase history, and online click-stream data.

Figure 5.2 illustrates a segmentation result generated from a hypothetical group of customers' shopping patterns[11]. The resulting segments are plotted as circles, where the axes represent the number of visits (x axis), the average spend per visit (y axis) and number of customers in that segment (circle size). Likewise, we are able to view the segments by their behavioral attributes (see Figure 5.3).

[11] These may include a combination of demographic attributes of customers such as age, gender, geography, income, previous purchases, purchase locations, mode of transaction, response to promotions, complaints, etc.

Understanding segmentation results can enhance the development of relevant shopping campaign models aimed at

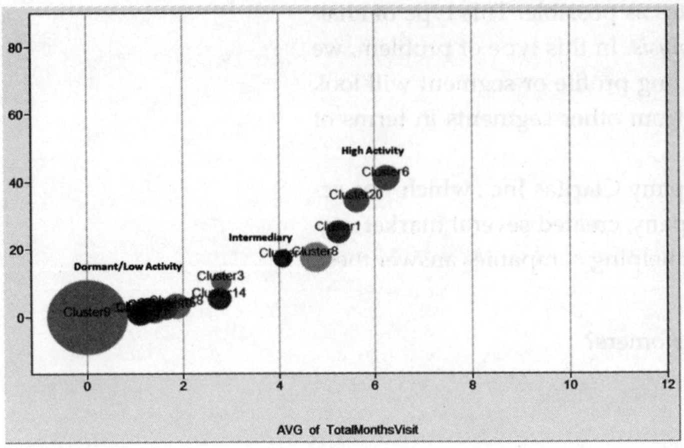

Figure 5.2: An illustrative visualization of a cluster analysis by number of visits (x axis), customer value (y axis), and number of customers per segment (circle size). Each segment represents a combination of attributes found to be representative of a unique behavior of interest.

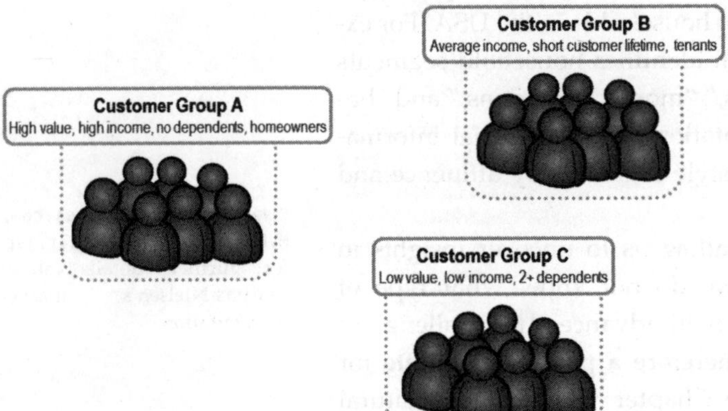

Figure 5.3: Example of three customer segments by applying a data-mining clustering algorithm that results in different behavioral attributes.

targeting customer groups. The number of clusters to opt for and how the cluster information is used depends on the required personalization level. For niche clientele companies, small and homogeneous groups of customers are needed, while for mass consumer companies a small number of large segments can suffice.

Another factor that affects the type of clustering is the diversity of customer behavior. Understanding customer behavior in a highly diverse population often requires using micro-segmentation, where each segment consists of very similar customers. Such segments might also be small in size. For example, a large retailer might consider each store separately and create store-specific segments. In contrast, for mass marketing at a non-personalized level (such as a billboard advertisement), clustering based on geographical information can help reveal the overall features of customers in a particular region.

Segmentation is also useful for monitoring campaign effectiveness in terms of migrating segments. Figure 5.4 illustrates a potential migration outcome after conducting a targeted campaign. We see that following the campaign, customers from some segments migrated to other segments.

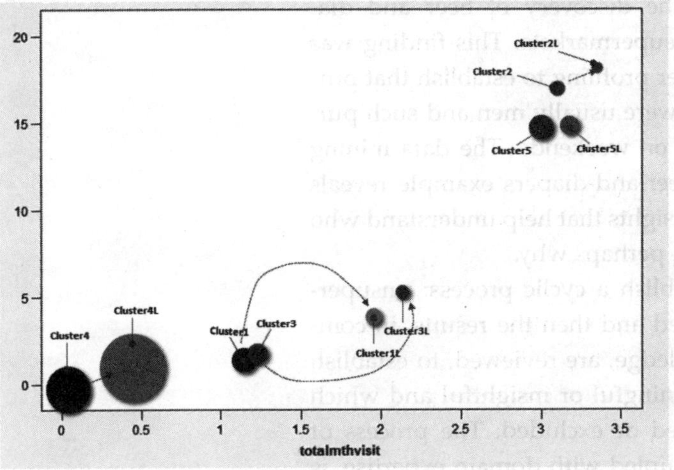

Figure 5.4: Schematic of migration results of segments in Figure 5.2 due to targeted campaigns.

Supervised classification methods are another set of data mining techniques useful for understanding the characteristics and behavioral patterns of customer segments. With classification methods, we pre-specify general types of customers by some dimension of interest, such as "high, medium, or low spenders", and then find the profiles of customers who fall into each of these categories.

We therefore prefer classification methods that create understandable relationships between segments and customer profiles. Two popular choices are *classification trees* and *regression models*. Classification trees produce automatically generated business rules that relate customers' profiles to the business question of interest. The resulting business rules can then shed light on the differences between individuals who fall into different categories.

Logistic regression provides information about what profile attributes distinguish between different segments, and the magnitude of the difference. For example, "high spenders are on average five times more likely than low spenders to purchase on weekends."

A third data mining approach to customer analytics is *market basket analysis* or *association rules*. Here the purchase history of each customer is used to learn which items are typically purchased together. A next step is to combine the results of the market basket analysis with the customer segmentation (clustering) results to figure out which customer segment tends to purchase certain combinations of products.

The classic example is the discovery of beer and diapers purchased together at supermarkets. This finding was then combined with customer profiling to establish that purchasers of beer and diapers were usually men and such purchases tended to take place on weekends. The data mining customer analytics in the beer-and-diapers example reveals not only patterns, but also insights that help understand who generates such patterns, and perhaps why.

A best practice is to establish a cyclic process: unsupervised segmentation is applied and then the results, in combination with domain knowledge, are reviewed, to establish whether the results are meaningful or insightful and which attributes should be included or excluded. The process of automated segmentation, coupled with domain expertise, is periodically repeated to reveal changes and new patterns and insights that might occur over time. This is depicted in Figure 5.5.

The expected outcomes of such approaches are increased wallet share, customer acquisition and retention. This includes increasing existing customers' spending and frequency of visits, improving customer satisfaction, retaining high value customers and maximizing the acquisition of high potential customers, and finally, acquiring more customers with the same behavioral and spending profiles as existing high value customers.

Beyond "The Customer"

We have used the term "customer" throughout this section, but the term can refer to any object of interest, from individuals in non-commercial settings such as medical patients, to non-individual entities such as financial transactions and in-

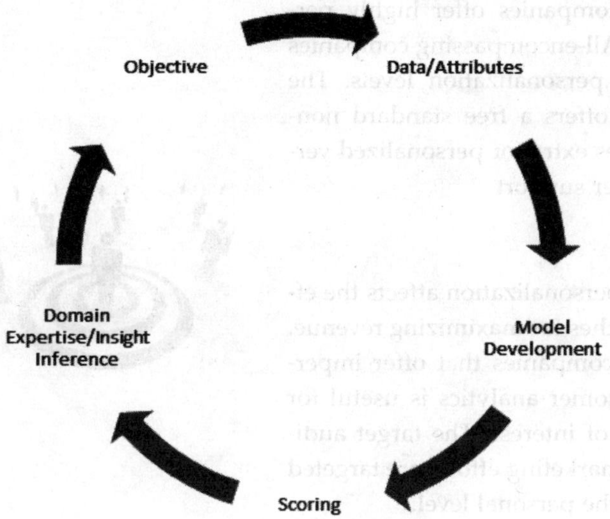

Figure 5.5: Best practice approach for model development and for integrating the model with domain expertise for process refinement.

surance claims. The same data mining approaches apply to all these settings. For instance, an old age home might apply data mining methods to the database of residents, including health profiles and other behavioral details, to better understand the different segments and their different needs.

5.2 *Targeting Customers*

I KNOW HALF OF MY MARKETING BUDGET IS WASTED. I JUST DON'T KNOW WHICH HALF.

— William Lever (1851–1925)
Industrialist, Philanthropist and founder of Unilever

The customer type spectrum described earlier, ranging from niche clientele to mass consumer populations, can be considered from the point of view of the personalization of the product or service being offered. In mass consumer companies, the product or service is not at all customized to the individual customer or even to customer segments; all customers receive an identical product or service. For example, low-cost airlines offer an identical product: a seat in an airplane on a given route.

In contrast, niche clientele companies offer highly personalized services or products. All-encompassing companies combine products of different personalization levels. The freemium model, for instance, offers a free standard non-personalized service, and charges extra for personalized versions, such as improved customer support.

Targeted Marketing

The level of product or service personalization affects the effectiveness of marketing approaches for maximizing revenue. In the case of mass consumer companies that offer impersonal products or services, customer analytics is useful for better targeting the population of interest. The target audience is seen as a whole, so that marketing efforts are targeted at the mass level rather than at the personal level.

In this scenario, it is not cost-effective to personalize marketing efforts, since the products or services are not customized in any way. The effectiveness of a marketing strategy in this case is driven by the ability to maximize the number of customers who buy in, while minimizing marketing costs.

Companies such as low-cost airlines target their potential customers by treating them as a whole. Banner ads and email promotions are not tailored to individuals. Customer analytics is used for market research and concentrates on figuring out *what product or service to offer*. For instance, a no-frills retailer can use historic data on trends to predict future demand, in order to decide what products to offer during different times of the year.

The relationship between customer analytics and marketing efforts is bi-directional, in that the results of mass marketing efforts can be used to further deepen the understanding of the mass consumer audience. For example, if advertising on billboards does not lead to sales (as can be ascertained by coupon codes posted on the advertisement), it gives an indication that either the advertised product is not of interest to the intended audience, or else the advertising medium is ineffective for this type of audience.

A different possible outcome, where advertising leads to buy-in by a completely unexpected segment of the population, can also greatly enhance the company's "know thy customer." All these cases provide customer information that can then be used to modify marketing and product offering strategies.

As we move away from impersonal mass consumer products and services towards all-encompassing companies that provide a wider range of products, and even further to companies offering highly personalized products or services, customer-specific targeted marketing becomes more effective.

In fact, as markets become richer in companies that provide personalized products and services, customers demand more personalized communication. In such environments, the success rate of mass marketing steadily declines and personalized marketing increases.

Targeted marketing in the personalized context means offering each customer the most appropriate product. Given that behavioral insight can be derived from customer databases using data mining algorithms, the next question is whether targeted marketing can be based on these insights to optimize response and buy-in. The usage of data mining methods for targeting marketing at the individual level allows addressing business questions such as:

- Which product should Amazon.com recommend to which customer?
- Which customer should Citibank offer a credit card to, and what type of credit card should be offered?
- What movies should Netflix.com recommend to which customer?
- Which news item should Yahoo! prominently display on its website to each user?
- Which song should personalized radio stations such as Pandora and Last.fm suggest to a listener?

The level of personalization in the marketing effort depends not only on the level of product personalization, but also on the marketing objective. In all-encompassing companies that cater to a combination of mass consumer segments as well as to more niche audiences, a common marketing goal is to upgrade mass customers to more loyal customers or to niche customers. The personalization level still might be lower than the white glove service level received by niche clients, but it would be more personalized than that offered to mass customers.

For example, a hotel chain might send a discount coupon for a certain weekend to a customer who will be celebrating an anniversary on that weekend. While the customer is not a VIP, this coupon might increase their loyalty to the hotel chain. A bank might offer a personalized service to customers arriving at the ordinary non-VIP counter, suggesting products of benefit to the customer, based on his/her banking profile. The personalized service may increase the loyalty of the customer, so that customers may upgrade to VIP customers by moving more wealth from other banks.

Personalized Recommendations and Ads

What if you could offer your customers exactly *what* they want, *when* they want it, even if they were not aware that they wanted it?[12] Customers are expecting, and indeed demanding, a personal experience where they are not treated as simply one of many. They expect organizations and companies to spend the time and effort to understand their individual requirements, and to cater to them in a personalized fashion.

[12] See "Target Knows You Better Than You Know Yourself" `jezebel.com/5886253/target-knows-you-better-than-you-know-yourself` - accessed 5th September, 2012.

Companies have responded by customizing marketing and advertising strategies. For example, when using Google's gmail service, the ads displayed in the right-hand column are based on the content of the relevant email message. Another example is the customized coupons that stores such as Target send to their customers, or coupons that customers receive immediately with their receipt after paying the cashier. Companies also personalize customer experiences by deploying online recommender systems. Examples include Amazon.com's "customers who purchased this item also purchased these items", movie recommendations by Netflix.com, and more.

In order to give a better understanding of the complexity of personalization, consider a company that reaches out to its customer base through emails, phone calls, mailers and flyers promoting various products through different types of promotional offers on these products (see Figure 5.7). Let us assume that this company has 8 communication channels (email, phone calls, flyers, mailers, etc.), 5 different promotional offers and only 4 products.

This seemingly limited number of components in fact amounts to 160[13] possible campaigns per customer. If we increase the number of products from 4 to 100 we now have

[13] Channels × offers × products.

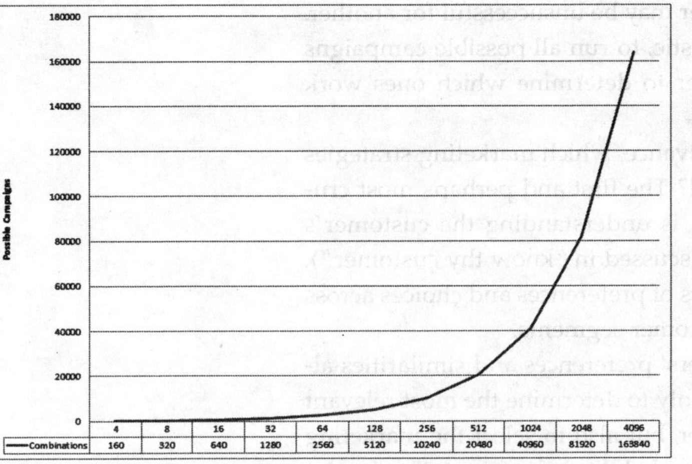

Figure 5.6: Setting the number of channels to 8 and the number of promotions to 5, we plot the increase in possible campaigns per individual customer (taking into consideration the channel, offer and product) as the number of products increases from 4 to 4,096. The increase in complexity is exponential.

4,000 campaign options per customer. The number of combinations increases quickly and significantly when considering the full range of products and communication channels as illustrated in Figure 5.6. Choosing the best combination for each customer is therefore not a trivial task. We discuss operational aspects in Section 7.2.

Figure 5.7: Driving value from customer relationships is getting increasingly complex due to the increase in products, channels and offers. There is a need to identify the right product through the right channel with the right offer for the right customer.

Personalized Marketing

The goal of any marketing campaign, in addition to increasing general awareness, is to achieve positive response from customers. When faced with an ever-increasing number of possible campaigns, how do we know which ones have a higher chance of success? In personalized marketing "success" is customer-specific, so that a marketing strategy that is successful for one customer may be unsuccessful for another. It is not possible, nor realistic, to run all possible campaigns for each customer in order to determine which ones work best for him/her.

How do we know, in advance, which marketing strategies will prove most successful? The first and perhaps most crucial step in this paradigm is understanding the customer's profile and behavior (as discussed in "know thy customer"), and uncovering the insights of preferences and choices across those specific types of customer segments.

Understanding customers' preferences and similarities allows an organization not only to determine the most relevant products for each customer, but also to select the marketing channel with the highest probability of success. The fundamental difference between traditional marketing approaches and the data mining approach is the latter's focus on harnessing the hidden knowledge from across the entire customer base to provide more targeted decisions and choices for future actions.

As technology advances, the level of personalization can be further enhanced. For example, mobile technology now allows the addition of geospatial information to other behavioral data, thereby enabling the targeting of customers based on their location. Customers are offered a product that is relevant not only to their profile, but also to a specific time and place. For example, while walking near a Starbucks branch, a "2 for 1 coffee" promotion is sent by SMS to a client who belongs to the 'impulsive coffee drinkers' customer segment.

Both in mass consumer products and in personalized marketing, the relationship between "know-thy-customer" and marketing efforts is bi-directional. The results of a personalized campaign can then be used to improve knowledge about individual customers. Macys.com[14] is an example of a mature retailer that incorporated analytics to increase customer insight for cross/up-sell by ending the "one size fits all" email marketing approach.

[14] Copyright ©SAS Institute Inc. Cary, NC, USA www.sas.com/success/macys.html.

Personalization Beyond Marketing

The ability to understand and target individuals does not end in the realm of marketing. An additional use is in improving operations, for example an international bank which wanted to improve its ability to collect credit card late payments, while minimizing its operational collection costs.

By clustering the credit card customer database, the bank was able to identify the different types of late credit card payers: Customers who are usually late and need to be called and reminded, those who just need an automatic reminder, and those who "just forgot" and pay by the next cycle. This understanding allowed the bank to greatly improve the collection strategy by optimizing for each customer the channel with the highest chance of success in payment collection, while minimizing the bank's operational cost. Most remarkably, the bank realized that there were 50% more self-cure customers, who would pay back the amount owed without any reminder whatsoever and that 50% of those that needed to be reminded could be contacted through an automated call system rather than by a human operator.

Personalized targeting is useful in many applications that are less revenue driven. Social welfare and rehabilitation organisations are exploring the use of personalized strategies to target individuals most likely to benefit from the service offered. Los Angeles County in the USA measures the costs and benefits of providing social welfare services to indigent adults and avoids duplicating services without compromising privacy[15].

Florida's Department of Juvenile Justice applies data mining methods to the database of juvenile offenders to identify those at risk of committing a crime and sends them to tailored treatment programs[16]. Institutions offering online education, such as University of Illinois at Springfield[17], are beginning to explore the use of customer analytics to improve learning outcomes of students by tailoring the most effective learning environment for different students.

Similar uses can be found in healthcare. Recently, researchers at Children's Hospital in Boston have devised a system for detecting emergency room patients who are likely to be victims of domestic abuse[18]. Several hospitals are also exploring personalized medical treatment, based on historic patient treatment and outcome data[19]. Finally, the U.S. Internal Revenue Service (IRS) uses their predictive analytics tools and applications as a first step in investigating potential tax evasion, fraud, under-reporting, tax preparer noncompliance, and money-laundering[20].

[15] Copyright ©SAS Institute Inc. Cary, NC, USA www.sas.com/success/lacounty_analytics.html.

[16] www.govtech.com/health/Florida-Adopts-Forecasting-Technology-to-Target.html.

[17] news.uis.edu/2011/05/uis-part-of-ground-breaking-study-aimed.html.

[18] www.childrenshospital.org/clinicalservices/Site1856/mainpageS1856P4.html.

[19] www.sas.com/success/louisville.html.

[20] www.accountingtoday.com/news/IRS-SAS-Analytics-Combat-Fraud-61081-1.html.

Relevant Data Mining Techniques

As in the case of "know thy customer," the personalization level determines the data mining tools to consider. The main difference is that the context of target marketing is focused on prediction, whereas "know thy customer" is focused on understanding. With the predictive priority in mind, we consider data mining techniques that produce predictions that can then be used for recommendations, marketing or other business actions.

Supervised methods (classification and prediction) are a key tool in personalized target marketing. They can be used to generate customer-level predictions based on the individual's profile ("Will a particular loan seeker default?", "How likely is this new customer to be a high spender?," "How much cash will the customer withdraw from the ATM?"). Note that this use is different from the "know thy customer" case. In the latter case, supervised methods are used to detect the main customer profile attributes that separate customer segments of interest ("What characterizes the average loan defaulter compared to a non-defaulter?," "How do low spenders differ from high spenders?").

In the targeting context, we are interested first and foremost in the predictions. Hence, a wide range of classification methods can be considered, including "blackbox" methods[21] and ensemble methods. Supervised methods can also be used to generate overall, non-personalized predictions by applying them to aggregated customer data. For example, to predict the number of cash-outs in an ATM, we can apply supervised methods to data that are aggregated at the ATM level, rather than use the individual transaction-level or customer-level data.

[21] Blackbox methods refer to algorithms in which it is difficult or impossible to determine the relationship between the input and output, that is, between the measurements and the predictions.

Another data mining technique used for highly personalized targeting is the recommender system. This is used in applications that require real-time differentiated customer experience such as online shopping. A customer's purchase history and current browsing behavior is used to generate real-time predictions of products or services that the customer may be interested in; these in turn provide immediate individual recommendations. Online advertising today is mostly based on creating personalized ads. Google Ads, for instance, uses information from email messages in Gmail account owners to determine which ads to display adjacent to their email. This level of personalization greatly differs from the early days of online advertising, when the same banner ad would be shown to all users.

For mass-consumer applications, forecasting methods are popular. They are used for projecting the future average or overall behavior of a large consumer population such as daily demand, hourly traffic, average refund amount, and monthly sales.

5.3 *Project Suggestions*

Customer analytics is about the identification of usable patterns for customer understanding and prediction. The first and primary focus in every project is defining an objective, hypothesizing possible outcomes as well as identifying measurable ROI. Note that the hypothesized outcome may in reality differ from the actual outcome, due to the nature of the data.

Project 1: Online Sales Prediction

We recommend using the following data on product online sales within a project. However, the suggested project outline can be applied to similar datasets. The sales data, publicly available for download from `www.kaggle.com/c/online-sales/data`, originate in a competition for predicting product monthly sales.

The dataset contains the following information

> The first 12 columns (Outcome_M1 through Outcome_M12) contain the monthly online sales for the first 12 months after the product launch. Date_1 is the date on which the major advertising campaign began and the product was launched. Date_2 is the date on which the product was announced and a pre-release advertising campaign began. Other columns in the data are features of the product and the advertising campaign. Quan_x are quantitative (numerical) variables and Cat_x are categorical variables. Binary categorical variables are measured as (1) if the product had the feature and (0) if it did not.

Project objectives

1. Explore the data and identify correlations between the attributes. Similarly, assess data quality and missing values.

2. Consider adding calculated attributes derived from the attributes provided.

3. Apply segmentation to cluster the products and interpret the results. Is there any natural division among the products that sold more than others?

4. Devise a prediction strategy to predict product sales one month[22] after launch.

5. What are the underlying attributes identified?

[22] This could be more than one month.

As a final stage, results should be concluded and presented in a short report and a 10-minute presentation. The results should include information as to:

- What was learned at the various stages of the analysis?
- What was the identified insight? Are you able to identify any customer- or product-related behavior(s)?
- What is the business value of the insight and how can it be incorporated?

Project 2: Exploring Customer Socio-Demographics

Suppose you are an analytics champion at a retail company selling expensive high-end jewellery. In this project, you have been tasked with exploring the potential of a dataset that includes census information for integration into a customer analytics implementation at your company. In particular, your company is interested in discovering the relationship between socio-economic factors and income, so as to be able to identify high-income customers without acquiring knowledge about their actual income.

The data for this project can be downloaded from `www.causality.inf.ethz.ch/data/CINA.html`. The abridged description of the data (including the original contest task):

> CINA (Census Is Not Adult) is derived from census data (the UCI machine-learning repository Adult database). The data consists of census records for a number of individuals. The causal discovery task is to uncover the socio-economic factors affecting high income (the target value indicates whether the income exceeds 50K). The 14 original attributes (features) including age, workclass, education, marital status, occupation, native country, etc. have been coded to eliminate categorical variables. Distractor features (artificially generated variables, which are not causes of the target) were added.

Project objectives

1. Explain how the discovery of a relationship between high income and socio-economic factors can be used strategically by your company.

2. The contest language includes the word *cause* ("The causal discovery task..."). Do these data support inferring causality? Would a discovery of association be sufficient for strategic implementation?

3. Explore the data using charts and tables to examine association between the income level and the other information. Highlight promising measurements.

4. What types of data mining techniques are suitable for predicting income?

5. What are the challenges in identifying this relationship? What are the challenges of different methodologies?

6. What are the underlying attributes that are most related to high income?

7. What else can be done with the data?

As a final stage, results should be concluded and presented in a short report and a 10-minute presentation. The results should include information as to:

- What was learned at the various stages of the analysis?
- What was the identified insight?
- What is the business value of the insight and how can it be incorporated?

6 Social Analytics

The era of social media has created a completely new, rich source of publicly available *unsolicited* customer feedback. Let us begin by defining the term social media. The official *Merriam-Webster Dictionary* definition of social media is:

> *Forms of electronic communication (as websites for social networking and microblogging) through which users create online communities to share information, ideas, personal messages, and other content (as videos).*

The Wikipedia article on "social media" notes that

> *Social media includes web-based and mobile technologies used to turn communication into interactive dialogue.*

We use the term *social media* to refer to any online medium that includes user-generated content in any form. This definition obviously includes platforms such as Facebook and Google+, user blogs such as WordPress and Blogger and micro-blogging sites such as Twitter and Tumblr. It also includes company user forums and public community forums and newsgroups. But more importantly, our definition also includes websites that have some social networking features, a very large proportion of websites. The Merriam-Webster online dictionary itself contains user comments, and therefore falls under our definition of social media. News websites include articles by bloggers (such as the NY Times website that contains a large section of blogs [1]), and some contain user comments. Google maps includes photos posted by users. Many websites include Facebook plug-ins, "like" or "+1" sharing buttons, or "email a friend" option.

[1] `www.nytimes.com/interactive/blogs`

In addition to data publicly available on social network websites, companies also gather information on personal social network data of customers and other Facebook users by using the Facebook API, creating Facebook Applications, or deploying Facebook Connect. These technologies enable users to share their information with third party websites and applications of their choice. According to the Facebook Developer blog:

> Hundreds of companies have leveraged these APIs, allowing users to dynamically connect their identity information from Facebook, such as basic profile, friends, photo information and more, to third party websites, as well as desktop and mobile applications... Facebook Connect is the next iteration of Facebook Platform that allows users to "connect" their Facebook identity, friends and privacy to any site. This will now enable third party websites to implement and offer even more features of Facebook Platform off of Facebook

A vast amount of data is therefore available to many companies on customers, non-customers and the connections between all the different entities.

6.1 *Customer Satisfaction*

Until not so long ago, organizations would solicit customer feedback on services or purchases through face-to-face, mail and phone surveys. A classic example is satisfaction surveys by airlines, where prior to landing, an air hostess would request selected passengers to fill out feedback forms regarding their satisfaction from the level of service rendered during the flight. More recently, email, Internet and mobile surveys have become the most popular tool for soliciting customer feedback. Companies might request a client to complete an online satisfaction survey after using their services or after a purchase. Meru Cabs, India's largest radio-taxi service, uses text messaging for soliciting customer satisfaction after each ride. The company sends a text message to riders who booked a reservation using their mobile phone immediately after the taxi ride, asking about their experience. The customer responds by replying to the text message.

While the technology has changed, a key similarity is that these methods of intelligence gathering are *solicited* (the customer is approached by the company) and are limited to the exact questions posed in the survey. Similar to "univariate analysis" described in Section 5.1, the choice of solicited information is done using a relatively small number of questions that are pre-identified as important to the company. In other words, we already know (or think we know) which questions are important in terms of correlating with an outcome of interest. With this approach, uncovering new unknown insights is limited.

IF YOU MAKE CUSTOMERS UNHAPPY IN THE PHYSICAL WORLD, THEY MIGHT EACH TELL 6 FRIENDS. IF YOU MAKE CUSTOMERS UNHAPPY ON THE INTERNET, THEY CAN EACH TELL 6,000 FRIENDS.

— Jeff Bezos (1964–)
CEO at Amazon.com

The Promise

Using our broad definition of social media, organizations have an enormous source of public, unsolicited customer feedback. Social media, first and foremost, translates to data — "free" data — that captures the moods, thoughts, opinions, likes and dislikes of existing customers and millions of potential customers. This ocean of unsolicited feedback is larger and broader by far than customer feedback solicited by companies.

Previously, capturing unsolicited feedback would have been an expensive or even an impossible exercise, because individuals are generally reluctant to share information directly with the service provider. With social media, however, a sufficient level of distance is formed, where customers feel more comfortable voicing their opinions and experiences. For example, in most cases a customer may be more inclined to complain on a public forum or share their experience and opinion online rather than providing the same feedback directly to the company representative. Internet users freely and openly share personal sentiments, opinions and complaints, either behind anonymous pseudonyms or even with their real identity (such as "real name™" reviewers on Amazon.com).

Another unique advantage of social media data to companies is the information about relationships between customers and even between customers and non-customers (potential customers). Without social media data, companies typically have data only on their one-to-one relationship with each customer. Social network data add a layer of connectivity information to the relationship of customers, non-customers and the company.

THE PRICE OF LIGHT IS LESS THAN THE COST OF DARKNESS.

— Arthur C. Nielsen (1897–1980)
Founder, ACNielsen

The Danger

The flip side of social media as a tremendous resource providing unsolicited customer feedback is that unsolicited content can not be controlled. Qantas Airlines' recent experience is an example of how social media should be handled with care. In October 2011, in an effort to promote a new brand under the name "Qantas Luxury", the company invited users to post on Twitter explaining why Qantas is associated with "luxury". The Twitter hashtag "#QantasLuxury" was then used to track these posts. The best tweet was promised a reward. Unfortunately, this promotion was aired shortly after the airline was grounded for several days, causing major inconveniences to passengers. The timing turned out to be disastrous. Tweets with hashtag "#QantasLuxury" poured in, but instead of praising the airline's luxurious feel, the tweets were rife with negative and often sarcastic commentary. The use of social media by Qantas backfired on its original goals. Even worse, it could not be switched off and was still ongoing at the time of our writing, almost a year after its launch.

Another danger lies in unauthentic customer reviews. The *New York Times* article "The Best Book Reviews Money Can Buy" (Aug 25, 2012) describes businesses of review writing that are purely commercial:

> Consumer reviews are powerful because, unlike old-style advertising and marketing, they offer the illusion of truth. They purport to be testimonials of real people, even though some are bought and sold just like everything else on the commercial Internet.

Mining such data and considering it authentic obviously creates a serious danger to true insight.

The Power of Social Media

In the past, online media replicated articles from traditional media. Today, the direction is reversed so that traditional media outlets often report news and updates originating from the online world. Social media has shifted power to the hands of Internet and mobile users. This change in power has caught many institutions off guard, from governments to public and private organisations. The Arab Spring, whose beginning was attributed to Mohamed Bouaziz in Tunis, was in fact the result of the subsequent online social outcry. On January 18, 2012, Wikipedia went offline for twenty four hours in protest against the proposed legislation of the Stop Online Piracy Act (SOPA) and the PROTECT IP Act (PIPA) in the USA. The reaction of the media and the acts' stakeholders to Wikipedia's blackout was mixed, but nevertheless widely reported. Millions of users became aware of the blackout and clicked on the link to learn more about it. As a result, the US Congress decided to freeze the two acts indefinitely. Internet users around the world have not only found their voice but they have also found the audience who listens.

In the business world, unsolicited company feedback now affects companies' operations and decisions. This shift in the role of social media as a key influential information source is depicted in Scott Cook's quote:

A BRAND IS NO LONGER WHAT WE TELL THE CONSUMER IT IS - IT IS WHAT CONSUMERS TELL EACH OTHER IT IS.

— Scott Cook (1952–)
Co-founder of Intuit Inc.

Social media has transformed the world, including the business world, into one led by public opinion, in which every individual with access to a computer and the Internet can make a difference. Customer complaints, which previously might have been directed at the company through company representatives, are now voiced publicly using social media. The public nature of social media has led companies to realize the importance of constant monitoring of social media and providing rapid response to user complaints and posts. One example is Best Buy's recent inability to fulfill online orders placed just before the holiday season. According to the *Wall Street Journal* (Dec 24, 2011),

> Angry customers flocked to Best Buy's online forums in recent days, complaining they received notices informing them that the purchases they had made weeks ago were cancelled.

The online buzz made the shortage immediately known to all, with traditional media quickly reporting on the events taking place online. Postings by customers on the company's online forums caused the company to quickly react. The *Wall Street Journal* describes one such case, where the customer not only received his order in time, but "a company vice president also e-mailed him an additional $200 gift card."

One of the authors experienced the power of social media in resolving a disputed charge with a large mobile telecommunication provider. While all efforts to resolve the issue using traditional channels (customer service, supervisors, and even the company ombudsman) dragged on and eventually failed, placing a complaint on a popular social media forum led to a rapid response from a social media customer care representative, who satisfactorily resolved the conflict and even politely requested the author to remove the post from the forum.

These examples illustrate the power that social media now has, and its increasing importance to companies. While these examples highlight social media as a source of concern for companies, we would like to emphasize that it encompasses an untold wealth of information for anyone seeking to explore its boundaries.

Beyond Customer Satisfaction

Online reviews on websites such as Amazon.com and TripAdvisor.com showcase the advertising role that social media plays. Customers and travelers often consult with such reviews before reaching a decision regarding a service or product to purchase. Some companies have learned to monitor and to react also to reviews. For example, some hotels make a point of responding to each review posted about their property on TripAdvisor.com. Responses include not only reactions to negative reviews, but also posts of thanks and appreciation to positive reviews. By engaging in this fashion with potential customers, the company can showcase their level of customer attention even before a transaction has taken place.

Social media has also affected media companies such as TV channels. One example is a TV series in India called Satyamev Jayate[2]:

> Satyamev Jayate, a reality show anchored by Khan that dealt with the issue of female foeticide in its first episode, saw huge support from viewers on social networking websites within hours of its broadcast on Sunday morning... Satyamev Jayate's website received 42,000 likes on Facebook by around 9pm. On Twitter, at least 3,800 tweets were posted on the subject.

[2] From article " 'Satyamev Jayate' a hit on social media", LiveMint.com, May 6, 2012.

The TV show solicits responses via social media during the episode itself ("Khan and his team have left no stone unturned in making sure viewers participate through phone messages. Satyamev Jayate's tweet said, *Thanks. SMS Y to 5782711 if the Rajasthan govt should set up a fast track court to tackle female foeticide."*). Such data are highly useful not only for purposes of advertising, but also for determining topics for future episodes.

6.2 *Mining Online Buzz*

The promise and danger of social media has captured the attention of companies. The main question that many companies now ask themselves is how to use the information obtained from social media for their (or their customers') advantage. From a machine learning point of view, data generated by social media typically include ratings and unstructured text, similar to data from email, documents, and computer logs. The first step is therefore *structuring* the text data, that is, converting the unstructured text data into structured form. Text mining, and especially sentiment analysis, is typically applied to the structured data. For some purposes, the results of the text mining are sufficient for generating the needed insights. For other purposes, another level of data mining techniques is required.

We now consider different uses of social media and discuss the data mining approach that supports these uses.

Rapid Information Dissemination

The most basic use of social media by companies is for pushing information out to customers in a timely fashion, thereby generating new data. Twitter is a popular choice, used for posting quick updates related to products or services.

An example is the use of Twitter by Bryna Corcoran, Hewlett Packard's social media manager and community management strategist, in the 2011 mad rush for HP's $99 TouchPad Tablet sale[3]. After the product sold out, the company set up a website that allowed customers to sign up and be alerted when more items were available. Corcoran posted frequent Tweets on availability of the product ("HP getting more early this week") at various locations. Her Twitter account gathered more than 30,000 followers.

[3] See more on HP's use of social media at www.hp.com/sbso/expert/printing/harness-social-media.html

Consumer-relevant information posted by a company to a social media site will likely lead to response posts by customers, as well as to further sharing of the post by customers with others (e.g., using the "share" button in Facebook or retwitting with Twitter). The information can then be shared even further by "second-order" users with further online fickle female fortitude"). Such data are highly useful not only for purposes of advertising, but also for determining topics for future episodes.

6.2 Mining Online Buzz

The promise and danger of social media has captured the attention of companies. The main question that many companies now ask themselves is how to use the information obtained from social media for their (or their customers') advantage. From a machine learning point of view, data generated by social media typically include ratings and unstructured [illegible] data from email, documents, and [illegible] [illegible] The first step is therefore structuring the te[illegible] [illegible] unstructured text data into st[illegible] [illegible] sentiment analy[illegible] [illegible] data. For some purposes [illegible] results of the text mining are sufficient for generating the needed insights. For other purposes, [illegible] level of data mining techniques is required.

We now consider different uses of social media [illegible] cuss the data mining approach that supports thes[illegible]

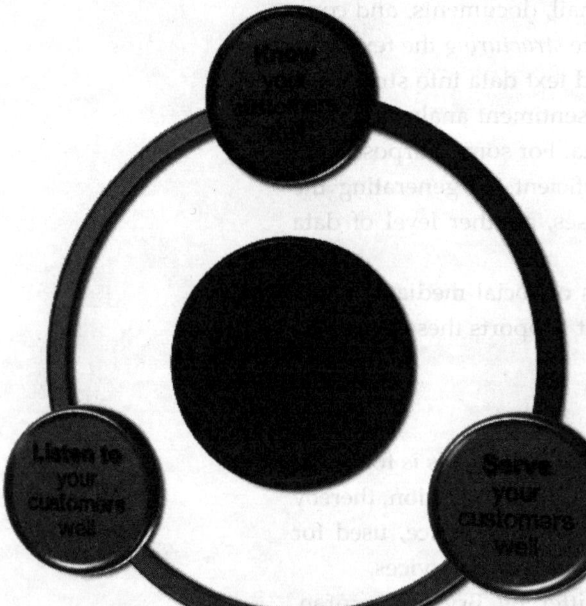

Figure 6.1: Social media can improve the various aspects of customer management. From rapid dissemination of information and response to unsolicited feedback ("Serve") to monitoring sentiments ("Listen") to enriching solicited customer data with social media data ("know thy customer").

Rapid Information Dissemination

The most basic use of social media [illegible] is for [illegible] ing information out to customers [illegible] ion, thereby generating new data. Twitter is [illegible] used for posting quick updates related to [illegible]

An example is the use of Twitter by [illegible] Hewlett Packard's social media manager and community management strategist, in the 2011 mad rush for HP's 500 TouchPad Tablet sale. After the product sold out, the company set up a website that allowed customers to sign up and be alerted when more items were available. Cosseran posted frequent Tweets on availability of the product ("HP getting more early this week") at various locations. Her Twitter account gathered more than 30,000 followers.

See more on HP's use of social media at www.hp.com/[illegible]

Consumer-relevant information posted by a company to a social media site will likely lead to response posts by customers, as well as to further sharing of the post by customers with others (e.g., using the "share" button in Facebook or retwitting with Twitter). The information can then be shared even further by "second-order" users with further online users, thereby creating a vast network of information. Mining these effects can lead to useful insights. The number of responses and the extent of sharing give an indication of the level of interest. Also useful are data regarding *who* shared the information and the feedback to the sharing. The text of comments and post sharing messages can contain important information that can be mined using text mining. Sentiment analysis can be used to ascertain the reaction of the audience to a post. This information can be used to learn about future postings and about possible next steps required. Link analysis (see Section 4.1) can be applied to the information on *who* commented or forwarded the information.

Improving Personalization

Customer analytics has recently started to include social media content, in an effort to extend "know thy customer" and customer targeting beyond self-collected or acquired data, so as to include unsolicited information. Two prominent examples are Google and Facebook, who actively mine their customers' online content, including email messages, posts, web searches, "likes" and any other content captured on their platforms. The companies mine the content, using text analytics, for their own purposes ("know thy customer") as well as for providing tailored third-party ads (personalization). Displaying customized ads further contributes to the richness of the data on a user's behavior — did the user click on a particular ad or not? What type of ads are clicked and when? — thereby adding even more information that can be used for further personalization.

Adding social media activity data to a customer's profile is possible when the customer's real identity can be linked to their social media username, as is the case in Google and Facebook. It is also common to find users posting identity data, such as an email address or mobile phone number, that can then be associated with their entry in the company's dataset. This information can be used for creating "sentiment scores" for improving personalisation such as for target marketing, as described in Section 5.2 (using segmentation and predictive analytics). A telecommunications company or bank might not want to contact an existing client with offers of new products or services if the client had just posted a comment stating how unhappy they are with the service. Sentiment analysis would have assigned this customer a negative sentiment score. The knowledge of negative comments provides the company with an opportunity to directly converse with the client to elevate their level of satisfaction, thereby strengthening their loyalty and perception of VIP treatment. Only then should the company contact them with further product solicitations. Similarly, if a customer posts positive feedback or indicates that they are currently exploring a product or service, text analytics can be used to identify this interest (or to create a positive sentiment score). This information can then be used to offer an upgrade or extension of their existing service/product or to recommend a relevant new product.

Monitoring Sentiments

Mining social buzz is also increasingly used by governments, political parties and other organizations, both commercial and non-commercial, that want to know what certain audiences think of them. While it is unclear whether online negative (or positive) sentiment truly reflects that of the offline world, it is clear that online sentiment affects what occurs in the offline world (as was the case with the Arab Spring).

Some companies and applications are based solely on gathering information from social media and reporting it to interested users. Applications such as Hitpad for the iPad are pitched as a quick and easy way to stay current and see what's currently "hot". The application mines and summarizes current trends of interest from social media and news websites. Companies such as SongKick.com, a website with a comprehensive and up-to-date database of music performances, mine social media as the basis of their operations. "Songkick's machine learning algorithms identify when any band on tour is mentioned in a blog"[4] and automatically notifies followers of the band as well as followers of similar bands.

[4] www.hypebot.com/hypebot/2008/03/songkick-debuts.html.

In Section 4.2 we described an application by TIBCO and Attivio that provided live information about Twitter user sentiment for different athletes in the 2012 London Olympics. A website displayed an interactive dashboard showing charts of positive and negative sentiments for the London Olympics athletes on Twitter[5]. During the Olympic games, the application displayed fresh information collected from Twitter every ten minutes on each athlete. This is an example of business intelligence applied to social media data.

[5] spotfire.tibco.com/demos/london-athletes.aspx

Internet users write posts about every possible product and service provider. They post comments, ratings and sentiments on large companies and service providers such as hospitals, universities, telecoms and consortia down to individual service providers including doctors, professors, and hairdressers. Companies can use text mining and sentiment analysis to capture the public's sentiments toward particular products or services, toward brands, or toward the company in general. Sentiments are also captured by monitoring the number of "fans" and "likes."

Organic, a digital advertising agency, provides its clients with measurements of sentiments in social media which are tracked over time. In particular, they look at indicators such as the number of Facebook fans and "likes" as well as compare changes in these indicators over time by computing measures of "velocity" and "acceleration."

Early Warning Systems

We have discussed how companies use social media to push information and notify customers of threats or other unexpected events, an area also known as horizon scanning. For example, some airlines use Twitter to notify passengers of flight delays.

In addition to generating independent data, companies also collect data from social media and user-contributed content to provide early warning. For example, an international company that regularly sends its employees around the globe for official business may constantly mine online media (social and other) to detect potential threats in the countries its employees are located in, or about to travel to. Timely detection of threats or warnings about terrorist attacks, political instability, natural disasters and social unrest allows for immediate SMS or email notification warnings to the employees. Governments and other organizations mine social and online data for reasons such as identifying disease outbreaks and spread.

In these types of applications, text mining and anomaly detection are the main tools. Anomaly detection includes predictive modeling and forecasting techniques. For example, comparison of forecasts of the number of daily tweets with #influenza to the actual count of tweets can indicate an outbreak. An example is Google FluTrends, which can be used to detect outbreaks of influenza faster than by using hospital visits or other traditional data:

> *We've found that certain search terms are good indicators of flu activity. Google Flu Trends uses aggregated Google search data to estimate flu activity.* (google.org/flutrends)

Google Trends (google.com/trends) allows obtaining (and visualizing) data on daily keyword search volume for keywords of choice (contingent on a minimal search volume). It presents this data as a set of charts and complements the volume information with news headlines related to that search.

Fraud Detection

Government agencies monitor and mine social data for detecting criminal acts. In addition, organizations such as insurance companies have recently begun to collect social network data to improve their fraud detection systems. Data from social media can prove highly useful for detecting fraudulent insurance claims. *Claims Magazine* contributor James Ruotolo, was quoted in the *Insurance Fraud News* article "Social media analytics exposing insurance fraud" (March 01, 2012):

> *"In the future, fraud detection engines will be based not just on claims and policy data, but also Facebook friends and Twitter posts."*

Some companies even mine their employees' social network data to detect fraudulent behavior such as taking sick-leave while in fact enjoying a vacation. Information such as photos posted by the employee or the employee's friends and even hotel check-in information might appear publicly on the employee's Facebook page or Twitter feed.

Learn Thy Competition

Mining the online buzz provides untold opportunities for competitive intelligence. In addition to gaining an understanding of what is being said about "my" products, a company can learn about what is being said about similar products being offered by competitors. Obtaining such detailed information is drastically simpler than entering the hairy world of corporate espionage. Comments and user feedback are in the public domain for all to read.

Data such as keyword search on Google, which can be obtained from Google Trends, can also be used to learn and compare products or services with competing brands. Companies can learn about their reputation over time, compared to their competitors. Companies can also monitor Twitter announcements by competitors, and see the user-base reaction to those announcements (recall the Qantas #QantasLuxury disaster).

The main tools used for "competition intelligence" in social analytics are text mining of user posts, and sentiment analysis for determining the tone of the comments. We also discussed the notion of network analytics and gave the example of networks of products (see Figure 4.2). Network analytics can be applied to ratings of different products, such as books on Amazon or movies on IMDB.com. Segmentation can be used to group similar products, thereby helping to detect competing items.

Testing Reactions to New Products

Online sentiments can be used as a test bed for new product or service offerings. For example, a library interested in offering book loan services through eBook readers might be unsure of the anticipated success/impact of adventuring into this new technology.

A traditional approach would be to conduct a survey and assess the opinions of a sample of readers. Social media offers two interesting improvements over the traditional survey approach. The first improvement is reaching a larger sample of readers through online or mobile surveys, through email or even by posting a poll on the library's Facebook page. This approach is cheaper and faster than traditional surveys. For instance, the second author of this book used a Facebook poll to decide between several book cover designs. The second improvement is collecting user feedback on similar services offered by other libraries or book stores (on book club forums, from customer reviews on on Amazon.com, etc.). The library can then gain insight not only on whether users liked or disliked the service, but also on what were the positive and negative aspects of users' experience.

Another example of using social media websites for evaluating new products before their launch, is the case of authors who use keyword search volume for choosing among multiple book titles. Google Trends is one tool for researching keyword popularity. Another similar tool is Google Insights for Search, which also includes forecasts for keyword search volume. An example is shown in Figure 6.2, showing the search volumes for the terms "business intelligence" (decreasing trend) and "business analytics" (increasing trend). Note that forecasting methods are used for generating the forecasts.

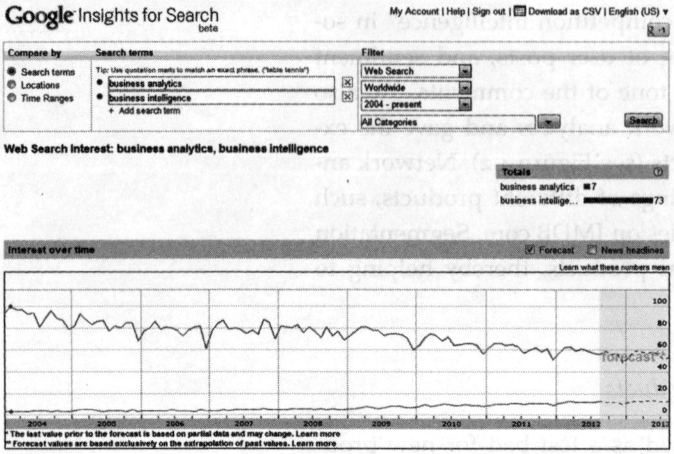

Figure 6.2: Google Insights for Search displays volume of keyword (or keyword combination) search, including forecasts. These can be used for making new product choices based on popularity trends.

Companies can also use social media to create as well as detect the "virality" of a new product. How quickly does the word spread about the product? How far does it reach — do posts by purchasers get re-posted, re-tweeted, and shared further? Aside from the volume of "buzz" (as determined by keyword search volume, Tweet volume, etc.) what is the sentiment conveyed about the product? Some companies choose to introduce a new product to a select group of people, who are then expected to post reviews and ratings on social media. For example, Amazon's "Vine™Voice" program is "an invitation only program that gives Amazon reviewers advance access to not-yet-released products for the purpose of writing reviews."[6] Responses to these reviews can then give an indication as to the level of interest and the type of interest that the product generates.

[6] www.amazon.com/gp/vine/help

Here too, text mining and sentiment analysis are useful tools. Networks analytics can be used to determine "influential" customers or reviewers who can then be approached for future testing or review.

6.3 *Project Suggestions*

Social analytics are used for extracting insight from social media data, either on their own or in combination with traditional data. The first step in any social analytics project is to identify a business need or opportunity for which the analytics will be used. As part of this process, it is useful to build scenarios of possible solutions, and how they will contribute to insight. To operationalize this process, it is important to define performance measures that are both relevant and measurable.

Project 1: Extracting knowledge from publicly available social network data

In this project, you will examine the type of insights that can be gained by collecting and merging data from multiple social networks. We rely on the scenario and data from a recent contest on CrowdANALYTIX.com in the area of tourism and travel. The data can be downloaded[7] from `www.crowdanalytix.com/contests/discovering-travel-decision-drivers-by-analyzing-tweets`.

[7] data access requires login.

The business context is described as follows:

Business Context:
Travel and Tourism industries are ideal for social media data analytics since many people make their travel decisions based on reviews on sites like TripAdvisor, Facebook and Twitter conversations. Gaining insight into this stream of data can be highly beneficial to the industry in making informed and targeted decisions on how to attract customers. A lot of companies are monitoring activities on social media sites to gather this information. Talking about a city or airport in a positive sentiment improves its image on the social sites.

Using advanced analytics and text mining techniques, we can use this data to uncover actionable insights and recommendations. Businesses can then connect with these customers with the right services at the right time.

Project Objective

Suppose you are the Chief Analytics Officer at an international airport in India. Your goal is to influence travel choices so that the airport becomes a destination of choice for transit or tourism.

1. Give an example of three recommendations that might be the result of a social analytics project.

2. List uses of social media for understanding international travelers' preferences.

3. What are the limitations of only using data from a survey conducted in the airport?

4. The data include Twitter data on over 50 keywords related to travel to India. What are text analytics methods that can be applied to these data? Consider the technology and what it will achieve.

5. Explore the data and report interesting patterns.

6. The contest goals were stated as:

   - Identify what motivates people to travel to India
   - Identify the main decision drivers for their travel
   - Identify activities while planning a trip to India or particular cities
   - Identify how travelers plan their trip.

   How can text analytics be used for approaching each of these goals?

7. How can the airport use social media other than by collecting data from such websites?

As a final stage, results should be concluded and presented in a short report and a 10-minute presentation. The results should include information as to:

- What was learned at the various stages of the analysis?
- What was the identified insight? Are you able to identify any attribute- or review-related behaviors that are relevant for predicting revenue?
- What is the business value of the insight and how can it be incorporated?

Project 2: Combining traditional data with user-ratings

For this project, consider yourself on the analytics team of a "daily deal" online firm that offers different types of discount vouchers on their website. The company is interested in maximizing the number of voucher sales. CrowdANALYTIX.com ran a contest with this theme in September 2012. The data to be used for this project are the competition data, although our guidelines below differ from the contest goals and rules. The full description of the context and goals for the contest is shown in Figure 6.3. The data can be downloaded[8] from `www.crowdanalytix.com/contests/modeling-daily-deal-market-offerings-to-maximize-profit/documents`. Below is an abridged description that is sufficient for our project scenario: [9]:

[8] data access requires login.

[9] from `www.crowdanalytix.com/contests/modeling-daily-deal-market-offerings-to-maximize-profit`

Data include the raw voucher attribute data for a single website's marketplace. The data is spread across varying locations in the US with differing demographic information. The data was web scraped from a single marketplace and is offered with social media Yelp.com reviews to add another layer of context.

Project Objective

1. The contest goal is to predict offering revenue based on the voucher attributes and the user ratings from Yelp.com. How can this analytics goal lead to business insight? Consider at least two ways in which accurate predictions can be useful in the context of the company.

2. How does the social media information differ from the data available on the website?

3. What other social media data might be useful for predicting revenue?

4. Explore the attribute and reviews data and in particular, examine the relationship between revenue and the other different measurements.

5. Which types of data mining techniques are potentially useful for predicting revenue?

6. Consider a realistic scenario where the data mining algorithm built on these data is being used for predicting the revenue from a voucher that will be launched the following week. What is the challenge when using the user ratings? How can they be used?

7. What are the advantages and limitations of integrating the ratings into a prediction model?

As a final stage, results should be concluded and presented in a short report and a 10-minute presentation. The results should include information as to:

- What was learned at the various stages of the analysis?
- What was the identified insight? Are you able to identify any attribute- or review-related behaviors that are relevant for predicting revenue?
- What is business value of the insight and how can it be incorporated?

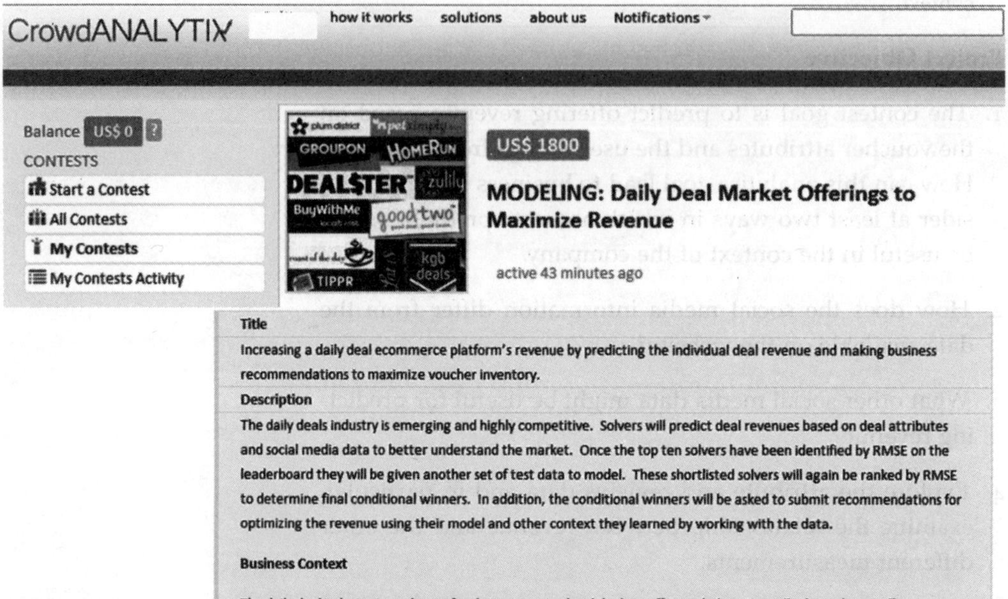

Figure 6.3: Screenshot of competition description on CrowdANALYTIX.com. With permission.

7 *Operational Analytics*

Consistent alignment of capabilities and internal processes with the customer value proposition is the core of any strategy execution.

— Robert S. Kaplan (1940-)
Baker Foundation Professor at Harvard Business School

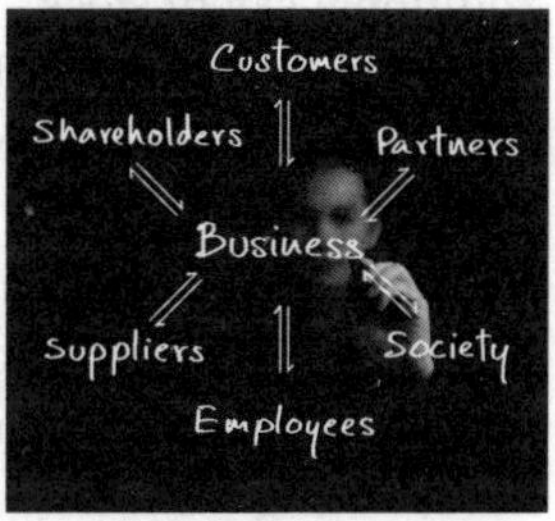

In previous chapters, we focused on customer-facing aspects of benefits that can be derived from implementing a business analytics approach within various organizations. However, business analytics and the underlying data mining techniques are not limited to these types of engagements.

In this chapter, we examine the benefits of business analytics in the context of operational aspects of a business. Marrying "front office" (customer-facing) business analytics with "back office" (internal) business analytics increases the benefits even further. We discuss the mutual benefits of linking operational insight leads to customer insight (see Figure 7.1).

For example, a magazine publisher can learn what content to publish and for which audience by using customer analytics. The same publisher would want to understand the *number* of issues to print and subsequently which resellers to distribute to. The operational goal is to maximize sales while minimizing the number of returned unsold issues, and thus wastage.

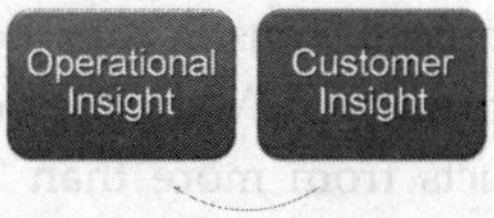

Figure 7.1: There is a strong and continuous link between the ability to uncover operational insight that leads directly to customer insight and uncovered customer insight that leads to further operational insight.

7.1 *Inventory Management*

Business analytics can play a significant role in improving an organizational operations, and in particular inventory management. The main goals in inventory management are minimizing holding costs and excess wastage, while ensuring the right items are available when needed. Achieving these goals leads to a reduction in inventory holding, while maximizing potential profit or up-time, and/or minimizing customer negative impact.

The application of business analytics to inventory management aims to achieve these objectives while addressing existing challenges. One example is the *Bullwhip effect*, also known as the Forrester effect[1]: companies add an inventory buffer called a "safety stock" (see image) to address unstable customer demand and operational challenges. Moving up the supply chain from the end-consumer to the raw materials supplier, each supply chain participant experiences increasing uncertainty in the level of demand and therefore requires additional safety stock.

[1] J Forrester's *Industrial Dynamics* (1961).

The Bullwhip effect describes the amplification in the demand uncertainty as one moves upstream in the supply chain and farther away from the customer. The result of this increasing demand uncertainty is that during periods of rising demand, down-stream participants increase orders, while in periods of falling demand, orders decrease or stop, thereby not reducing inventory.

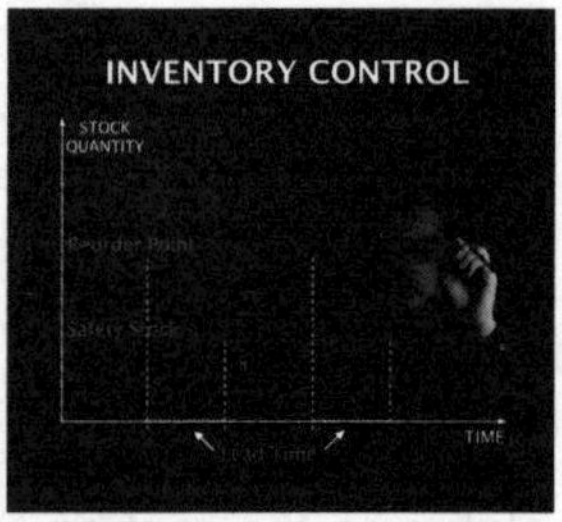

The application of business analytics techniques can be thought of as flattening out the Bullwhip effect as much as possible. The consequences of not addressing inventory challenges are an inability to adhere to consumers' demand, as occurred with the large retailer Best Buy during the 2011 Christmas holiday shopping season. The company notified online customers, just two days prior to the Christmas holidays, that their online order would not reach them on time[2].

[2] "Best Buy apologizes for web sales blunder", *Wall Street Journal*, Dec 24, 2011 `online.wsj.com/article/SB10001424052970204552304577116722465562402.html`.

Due to the cost of maintaining stock, the trade-off is between limiting inventory while maintaining optimal availability. To illustrate the magnitude of a business analytics approach, consider the Belgian pharmaceutical distributor and retailer CV Vooruit, which stores approximately 10,000 products from more than 200 suppliers in its main warehouse. The company was able to improve its service-level performance by 3%, reaching 97% of its target while increasing inventory turnover by five times. These results reduced stock-outs, which in turn increased profit. This was achieved by improving forecasts for their overall inventory stock levels as well as for individual drugstores.

Traditionally, the context of inventory management addresses questions by retailers such as Walmart or CV Vooruit regarding *when, where and how* to stock shelves, thus reducing costs and improving profits. However, we are able to expand the application to any scenario that consists of an inventory-like management system. For example, a cargo logistics operator needs to forecast the inbound and outbound cargo loads at its various ports of operations to plan the required optimal level and skill set of the staff.

Dnata, the largest airport terminal cargo operator in the Middle East, uses business analytics capabilities to forecast workloads, which helps streamline productivity and fine-tune resource requirements such as manpower, equipment and facilities to meet peak loads[3]. They were able to significantly increase productivity per man hour worked. Similarly, hospitals need forecasts for the number of in-bound patients to plan for the required number of beds as well as the number of doctors and nurses to man the wards.

[3] Copyright ©SAS Institute Inc. Cary, NC, USA `www.sas.com/success/dnata.html`

Figure 7.2 illustrates typical demand forecasting, where past behavior is used to forecast future values and the uncertainty in those values.

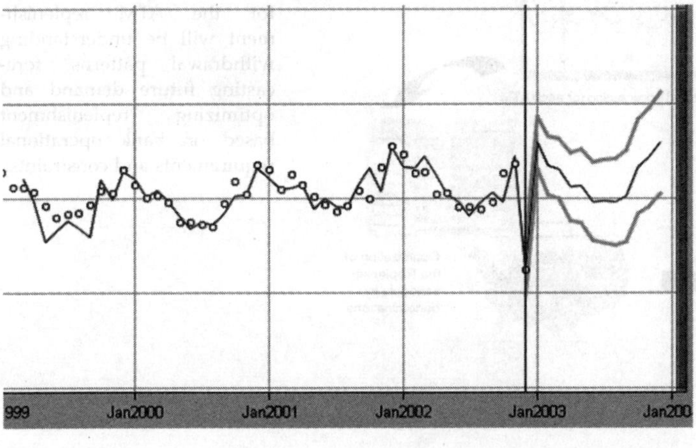

Figure 7.2: Forecasting techniques are applied to historical demand/supply data to identify trends and seasonality patterns that are then used to forecast future demand/supply. Forecasts are typically supplied alongside upper and lower bounds (prediction interval).

A more complete approach toward inventory management goes beyond forecasting the required stock level and type; it also integrates forecasts within a larger system that optimizes logistics, in order to achieve a holistic inventory management system.

The challenge of cash replenishment of ATMs or bank branches captures both aspects of inventory and logistics. The underlying objective is to minimize negative customer impact by assuring that ATMs are replenished on time, thereby avoiding a "cash-out" state where no money is left in the machine. A solution for avoiding cash-outs must simultaneously take into account the need to minimize the Bank's operational cost by minimizing the number of trips required to do perform replenishments. Reacting on an adhoc basis to the ATM cash levels lacks foresight and will result in a large number of last minute ATM replenishment trips.

It is imperative to understand customers' withdrawal patterns from the ATM network, taking into consideration compounded seasonal effects. With such data, it is potentially possible to be able to forecast (days in advance) what *will be* the withdrawal pattern. These forecasts provide the insight regarding *which and when* ATMs will reach a cash-out state. Subsequently, an optimization routine can build on the forecast results to generate an optimal replenishment schedule, based on operational constraints and actual withdrawal (supply based on demand). This process is graphically illustrated in Figure 7.3.

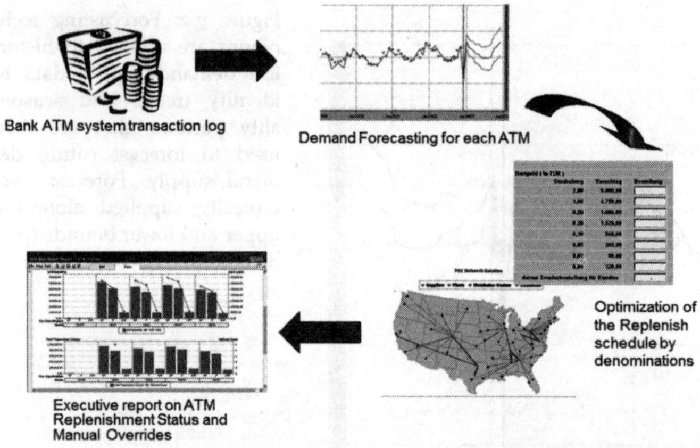

Figure 7.3: The process flow for the ATM replenishment will be understanding withdrawal patterns, forecasting future demand and optimizing replenishment based on bank operational requirements and constraints.

The data mining techniques used for achieving these types of goals are generally time-series forecasting followed by optimization. These systems operate by observing and analyzing behavioral patterns and are limited to the information provided. The business analytics solution must therefore constrain the data mining solution by operational requirements based on domain expertise. In the ATM replenishment case, one must take into account expected policy changes, bonus payouts and sporting events which all impact withdrawal patterns. Even with this added operational knowledge, one must always consider the "unknown unknowns", also known as "act of God" or "Black Swans," which are events that are unpredictable by humans and machines alike.

7.2 *Marketing Optimization*

We have extensively covered the areas of customer analytics in Chapter 5 and have briefly reviewed how these can be extended beyond direct customer engagement in Section 5.2. We now examine the operational aspect of a marketing engagement, considering that a typical marketing engagement has a set of limitations and requirements. Operational requirements may include:

- Limiting the number of customer contacts
- Limiting the number of household contacts
- Limiting the number of offers per campaign
- Staying within an overall budget
- Keeping the credit card budget low
- Not exceeding the call center volume capacity
- Limiting the number of email offers
- Limiting the amount spent on "low profit" customer segments
- Maximizing profit.

We return to our credit card example from Section 5.2, this time highlighting the operational aspect and how analytics can be driven to achieve an optimal strategic objective:

> *By clustering the credit card customer database, the bank was able to identify the different types of late credit card payers: Customers who are usually late and need to be called and reminded, those who just need an automatic reminder, and those who 'just forgot' and pay by the next cycle. This understanding allowed the bank to greatly improve the collection strategy by optimizing for each customer the channel with the highest chance of success in payment collection, while minimizing the bank's operational cost.*

We use a hypothetical small-scale example to illustrate the issues involved in a marketing optimization problem. Assume that a company is interested in running three different marketing campaigns: credit cards, resort rides, and hotel rooms. These will be offered to the existing customer base of nine individuals. We further assume that there are two simple business constraints:

- Each customer must receive an offer from exactly one campaign.
- Each campaign must target no more than three customers.

In Figure 7.4 we review a standard approach where campaigns are prioritized based on potential revenue. This standard approach assigns campaigns to customers who are likely to generate the highest profit. This is done by comparing customers in each campaign separately.

In our example, if we start with the credit card campaign, customers #1, 7, and 9 are selected, because they are expected to generate the highest profit. Then, for the next campaign, resort rides, we can only select from the six remaining customers (as the first three already received a credit card offer). Comparing expected profit from these six customers, the ride offer would be sent to customers #2, 3, and 4. Finally, the remaining three customers would receive the hotel room offer.

The allocation of customers to campaigns in the standard approach depends on the chosen sequence of campaigns. Such prioritization must be determined manually by the domain expert. In this example, given our constraints and the campaign prioritization approach, we achieve a potential profit of $655.

In Figure 7.5 we apply an alternative customer prioritization approach, whereby *for each customer* we select the campaign that has the maximum expected profit. This alternative strategy, while sensitive to the order in which customers are reviewed (decided by a domain expert), improves our potential profit by $60 to $715.

Finally, we demonstrate the results of an optimization methodology, which sets up the problem of matching customers to campaigns holistically, given the two operational constraints. Using optimization methods, the solution to this problem is illustrated in Figure 7.6.

The optimization approach identifies that sending a hotel room campaign to customer #4 allows sending a rides campaign to customer #9, thus yielding an *optimal* solution for maximum profit given the operational constraints. No allocation achieves a higher profit than that of the optimization approach (here, $745).

	Priority #1	Priority #2	Priority #3
Customer	Credit	Rides	Rooms
1	**100**	~~120~~	~~90~~
2	50	**70**	~~75~~
3	60	**75**	~~65~~
4	55	**80**	~~75~~
5	75	60	**50**
6	75	65	**60**
7	**80**	~~70~~	~~75~~
8	65	60	**60**
9	**80**	~~110~~	~~75~~

Profit = $655

Figure 7.4: In the standard prioritization strategy, customers are allocated to campaigns by separately examining each campaign, where the order of campaign consideration is pre-set. In this example, we first consider credit card, then rides, and finally hotel rooms. This ordering leads to an expected profit of $655.

In this example, we can calculate the optimal result manually by permuting the order in which we focus on customers and campaigns. Even in this small example, this can easily become overwhelmingly complex.

The secondary benefit of optimization systems is that the problem can be "flipped," allowing us to derive additional insight beyond finding the optimal customer-campaign allocation. In particular, we can explore the relationship between the operational constraints and the optimal output. We might discover that the optimal solution is not operationally optimal and therefore we might modify some constraints or even change conflicting objectives.

7.3 *Predictive Maintenance*

The traditional world of maintenance encapsulates two main forms: *reactive maintenance* and *preventive maintenance*. In the former, maintenance teams begin to resolve a disruptive event (an "asset failure") after a partial or total loss of functional performance. In other words, the functional perfor-

Customer	Credit	Rides	Rooms
1	100	120	90
2	50	70	75
3	60	75	65
4	55	80	75
5	75	~~60~~	50
6	75	~~65~~	60
7	80	~~70~~	75
8	~~65~~	~~60~~	60
9	~~80~~	~~110~~	75

Profit = $715 (increase of $60)

Figure 7.5: A prioritization strategy where campaigns are compared for each customer, and the most profitable is chosen. This strategy depends on an expert-based customer ordering. This strategy leads to an expected profit of $715.

Customer	Credit	Rides	Rooms
1	100	120	90
2	50	70	75
3	60	75	65
4	55	80	75
5	75	60	50
6	75	65	60
7	80	70	75
8	65	60	60
9	80	110	75

Profit = $745
(overall improvement of $90)

Figure 7.6: In an optimization strategy, the most profitable configuration of campaign and customer is selected holistically, while taking the constraints and objective into consideration. This approach leads to an expected profit of $745.

mance is already experiencing loss. Failure detection is based on *lagging reactive indicators*, which are measurements, such as sensor readings, indicating that complete failure has occurred. For example, when driving a car, a lagging reactive indicator of brake failure is complete loss of control. Recalls by companies are another example of reactive maintenance that relies on lagging reactive indicators.

The goal is to shorten the time from failure detection to intervention, as well as to maximize the ability to detect true events and to minimize false alerts. The latter two objectives are an effort to move from reactive to proactive. *Lagging proactive indicators* are measurements that indicate partial failure. In our brake failure example, a possible lagging proactive indicator is sensing a degradation in braking performance.

The next step is moving to pre-event notification, using *leading reactive indicators*. These measurements are early warning signs based on a divergence of some metric of interest from its target. For example, the gasoline gauge in a car is a leading reactive indicator for the event of an empty gasoline tank.

Preventive maintenance is based on maintenance cycles which are conservatively calculated and planned by the manufacturer of the equipment. Examples include routine elevator maintenance service, annual automobile inspection, and routine doctor visits. While these are leading proactive interventions, they may be both futile and wasteful. In fact, some cross-industry surveys estimate that a third of all preventive maintenance jobs are unnecessary.

It is sometimes possible to carry out reactive and preventative maintenance while equipment is in operation, but more frequently, equipment must be shut down for the maintenance period, thereby causing inconvenience and incurring losses.

The relationship between the leading and lagging indicators on the event timeline are illustrated in Figure 7.7. The earliest indicators, however, are *leading predictive indicators*, part of *predictive maintenance*.

Predictive maintenance (not to be confused with preventive maintenance) is based on analyzing the various conditions of a single asset (sensors, logs, ongoing operations) to *predict* when failures are likely to occur. This type of analysis involves assessments of the equipment during normal operation. Predictive maintenance relies on actual signals triggered by a single and specific piece of equipment, so that maintenance can be scheduled when necessary to minimize operations disruption. Such *leading predictive indicators* go farther

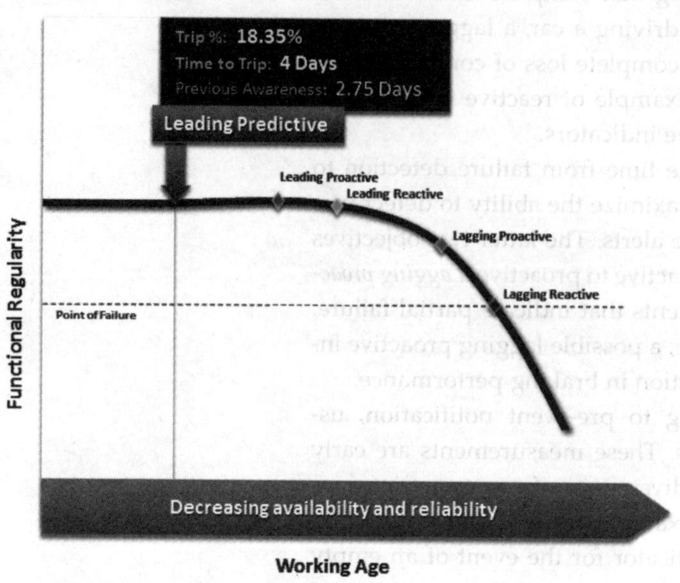

Figure 7.7: The objective of predictive maintenance is to improve asset availability, minimize unscheduled outages and avoid performance degradations and catastrophic failures by providing as much lead time as possible for a predicted failure.

than traditional methods, nearly tripling the time between notification and failure.

The capabilities of predictive maintenance lead ultimately to maintenance optimization, taking into account risk, required skill sets, required service parts and various other considerations, while minimizing maintenance costs and/or downtimes. It can also be applied strategically to optimize the maintenance strategy of assets, based on their real performance and condition. By analyzing and incorporating the combined conditions that led to past problems, maintenance schedules can be optimized to account for risk and required skill set with the end goal of minimizing operational costs and disruption and of maximizing performance and operating conditions.

The prediction of failure consists of two types: predicting failures that have occurred in the past, and predicting failures that have not yet occurred (in other words, predicting the ones that you know, and the ones that you do not know). In both cases, one must understand and label asset behavior based on different operational modes ("healthy," "somewhat unhealthy," etc.) to understand how the asset behavior fluctuates during normal operation. Once an asset begins to drift from a healthy to an unhealthy segment, the system should not only sound an alert but also suggest why the shift has occurred. This is similar to customer analytics, where we look at customers drifting from one segment to another. Similarly, unknown events might have precursors of unusual (abnormal) behavior to indicate a change in the normal mode of operation. Modeling normal behavior is traditionally done using methods such as survival analysis.

SR Technics Switzerland, a player in the aircraft maintenance and engineering market, uses predictive maintenance to help improve scheduling of aircraft maintenance. This approach was shown to enhance aircraft safety, reduce operating costs, and increase time savings.

While the application of predictive maintenance is potentially wide and varied, assets can be divided into three types:

- **Maintenance Cost:** Assets such as drills on oil rigs, aircraft, commercial satellite dishes and telecommunication tower relays, are heavy-duty, expensive and not easily replaceable or else replaceable at significant cost. Identifying potentially crippling failure is vital in ensuring continuous operation and longevity of such assets.

- **Downtime Effect:** Inexpensive equipment such as mobile phones or computers are usually not ideal candidates for predictive maintenance, as these types of assets are inexpensive and easily replaceable. However, the application of predictive maintenance becomes applicable when the respective downtime of this equipment creates a significant negative impact. For example, a server failure in a telecommunication call routing center would cause significant inconvenience to its subscribers. In these cases, it is the pre-emptive identification of failure, rather than the repair of the item, that is of primary concern.

- **Combination:** The third type of asset is a combination of the above asset types in terms of equipment cost and impact of failure.

7.4 *Human Resources & Workforce Management*

Employee-related expenses are the single largest cost category within any organization. And yet, companies do not manage their human resources with as much focus and investment in systems and processes as they do with office supplies and spare parts. Despite employees being the core of (almost) any organization, the amount of investment in analytics solutions for process improvement or insight discovery is fairly limited in HR and workforce related systems.

The types of challenges encountered in workforce management include employee-related operations, from staff scheduling and allocation, to employee churn, training and compensation.

Analytics in this field rely mostly on Excel spreadsheets and static reports for day-to-day operations. These can become daunting, especially for dynamic and last-minute changes. For example, when a cargo plane lands later than scheduled, a quick manpower rescheduling is required to accommodate the new arrival time. More advanced analytics, based on optimization, can lead to optimal solutions in faster time, taking into consideration all constraints and requirements. Figure 7.8 shows an output from an optimization system for staff allocation across several branches of a company, given each branch's requirements in terms of experience, skill set and budgetary constraints.

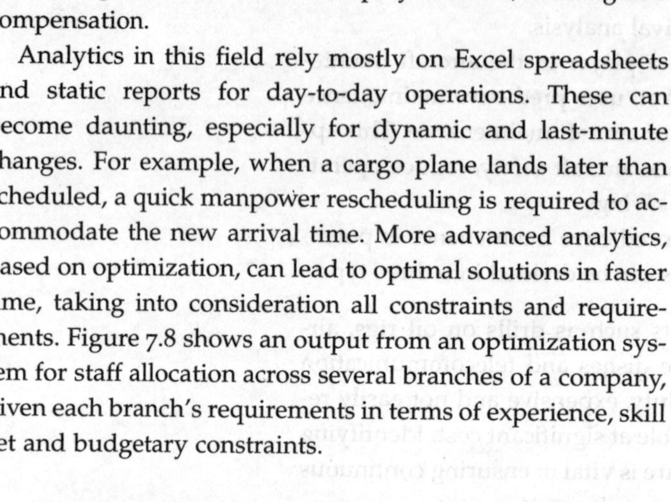

Figure 7.8: Example by SAS for optimal allocation of staff with different experience, skill set and salary to branches with assigned budget and requirements.

Key questions that arise when dealing with such workforce related systems are:

- What is the ability to explore restructuring scenarios and their implications before decisions are made?
- Which employees are critical? Which are likely to leave the

organization and why?

- How can the effectiveness of HR initiatives and their impact on organizational objectives be proven?
- Are these initiatives connected with the needs and objectives of the business units? Do they add value?

A current key question in many organizations is *who will leave, and why*. Knowing in advance about potential employee churn minimizes the risk of losing critical employees, key skills and top talent.

Operational workforce management is fundamentally similar to our previous scenarios, in that it is about identifying the *workforce gap* (demand minus supply) as well as what can be done about it (workforce planning). The required capabilities are based on forecasting and predictive analytics. An example of such planning comes from North Carolina Office of State Personnel[4], which focused on building its workforce by predicting departures, retirements and vacancies, and developing workforce plans.

[4] Copyright ©SAS Institute Inc. Cary, NC, USA www.sas.com/success/ncosp.html.

Applying analytics for workforce management requires integrating workforce data from multiple sources (subject to regulation and ethical considerations) for a holistic view and understanding of employees, similar to the approach that we described in customer analytics. This process enables a subsequent analysis of the workforce to understand strengths and vulnerabilities. It can also help understand and predict absenteeism, voluntary terminations, etc. Most importantly, such insight and predictability allow for better alignment of human capital with business objectives and direction. We can use analytics to optimize the workforce to pro-actively respond to change by finding the best possible solution, given a specific goal and constraints. For example, finding the optimal mix of hires, layoffs, training, and relocations to achieve a specific goal.

7.5 Project Suggestions

In the following section, we suggest two projects that focus on operational analytics.

Project 1: Managing University Resources

You are leading an initiative in a university, aimed at improving the efficiency of time spent by researchers. In particular, you want to reduce time wasted on writing proposals for research grants that are likely to fail. This project is motivated by a competition on Kaggle, based on data from the University of Melbourne. The data for this project are available at `www.kaggle.com/c/unimelb`.

The business context is described as follows on the competition website[5]

[5] `www.kaggle.com/c/unimelb`.

> **Business Context:**
> Around the world, the pool of funds available for research grants is steadily shrinking (in a relative sense). In Australia, success rates have fallen to 20–25 percent, meaning that most academics are spending valuable time making applications that end up being rejected.
>
> With this problem in mind, the University of Melbourne is hosting a competition to predict the success of grant applications. The winning model will be used by the university to predict which grant applications are likely to be successful, so that less time is wasted on applications that are unlikely to succeed. The university hopes the competition will also shed some light on what factors are important in determining whether an application will succeed.
>
> The university has provided a dataset containing 249 features, including variables that represent the size of the grant, the general area of study and de-identified information on the investigators who are applying for the grant.

Project Objective

1. Consider the operational goal as an optimization task. Define the objective function, the constraints, and the factors to be measured.
2. How do predictions of grant success feed into the optimization task?
3. Explore the data, and especially the relationship between grant success and other attributes.
4. What data mining methods are potentially useful for this task?
5. What is the difference, in terms of business insight, between obtaining accurate predictions of grant success and understanding the factors that determine success? How can each of these insights lead to business value?

As a final stage, results should be concluded and presented in a short report and a 10-minute presentation. The results should include information as to:

- What was learned at the various stages of the analysis?
- What was the identified insight? Are you able to identify any grant or researcher attributes that are relevant for predicting grant success?
- What is the business value of the insight and how can it be incorporated?

Project 2: Hospital Admissions

For this project, consider yourself a member of the analytics team in a hospital where you are charged with creating an analytical system to help plan for the number of beds required in the different wards. We use data from the Heritage Health Prize `www.heritagehealthprize.com/c/hhp/data`, a contest with the goal of predicting the number of days that inpatients or emergency room patients stay in the hospital.

The business context is described as follows on the competition website[6]

[6] `www.heritagehealthprize.com`

Business Context:
More than 71 million individuals in the United States are admitted to hospitals each year, according to the latest survey from the American Hospital Association. Studies have concluded that in 2006 well over $30 billion was spent on unnecessary hospital admissions. Is there a better way? Can we identify earlier those most at risk and ensure they get the treatment they need? The Heritage Provider Network (HPN) believes that the answer is "yes".

The winning team will create an algorithm that predicts how many days a patient will spend in a hospital in the next year. Once known, health care providers can develop new care plans and strategies to reach patients before emergencies occur, thereby reducing the number of unnecessary hospitalizations. This will result in increasing the health of patients while decreasing the cost of care. In short, a winning solution will change health care delivery as we know it, from an emphasis on caring for the individual after they get sick to a true health care system.

Project Objective

1. The contest goal is to predict length of stay in the hospital. How can this analytics goal lead to business insight? Consider at least two ways in which accurate predictions can be useful in the context of a particular hospital.
2. Explore the data, and in particular examine the relationship between length of stay and the other measurements.

3. What is the difference between predicting the individual patient length of stay, and forecasting the total number of patients in the hospital on a daily basis in terms of the business objective?

4. How would you forecast the number of patients admitted on a daily basis? What analytic techniques are potentially useful? What data are necessary?

5. How would you predict the hospital length of stay for each new patient? What analytic techniques are potentially useful?

6. Formulate the assignment of patients to beds as an optimization problem. Formulate constraints on number of beds and other relevant factors.

7. How would you combine the prediction, forecasting, and optimization as a holistic operations solution?

As a final stage, results should be concluded and presented in a short report and a 10-minute presentation. The results should include information as to:

- What was learned at the various stages of the analysis?
- What was the identified insight?
- What is the business value of the insight and how can it be incorporated?

Epilogue

Imagination is more important than knowledge.

— Albert Einstein (1879–1955)
Theoretical Physicist

Business analytics is a continuous journey on a path toward organizational enlightenment. It is the focus point of the never ending question "why?" and the pursuit of an answer. In the preface, we expressed our desire to guide you through a journey into the world of business analytics, exploring its contents, capabilities, and applications. As with any journey, there is a need for goalposts to mark one's progress. While we hope you have absorbed many take-away messages as goals along your path, the one most important message is also the simplest. This message, the eureka moment, is imagination. It is the realization that business analytics, while addressing minds actively engaged in the pursuit of business insight, is a Rubik's cube that can adapt and transform according to the needs and objectives of its users.

Business analytics is able to effectively transform business operations with improved efficiency, reduction of costs, increased profitability and improved customer (internal as well as external) engagement. The topics discussed in this book share a commonality; despite the variance in both domains and operations, when transforming an analytical procedure into a day-to-day process, the fundamental analytical techniques are the same. This flexibility captures an essential and important aspect of business analytics: it is only limited by the imagination of those who apply it. The key ingredient for business analytics is an inquisitive mind.

We hope that by reading this book, you have realized not only what you know, what you think you know, and what you knew you did not know, but also have glimpsed what you did not know you did not know. And we hope that you have gained an appreciation for the tools and approaches capable of reducing the unknown.

It is important to keep up to date on business analytics applications in various organizations, so as to expand your knowledge on possible implementations and to give you ideas for new directions. Conferences such as Predictive Analytics World and Predictive Analytics Summit bring together speakers and attendees interested in analytics specifically at the strategic business levels. To learn about latest data mining and data analytics techniques, recommended events are the *ACM SIGKDD Conference on Knowledge Discovery and Data Mining* and the *INFORMS Conference on Business Analytics and Operations Research*. Professional social networks comprise another useful knowledge and connectivity channel. LinkedIn groups such as Advanced Business Analytics, Data Mining and Predictive Modelling feature many members and discussions revolving around business analytics.

THE KEY INGREDIENT FOR BUSINESS ANALYTICS, IS AN INQUISITIVE MIND.

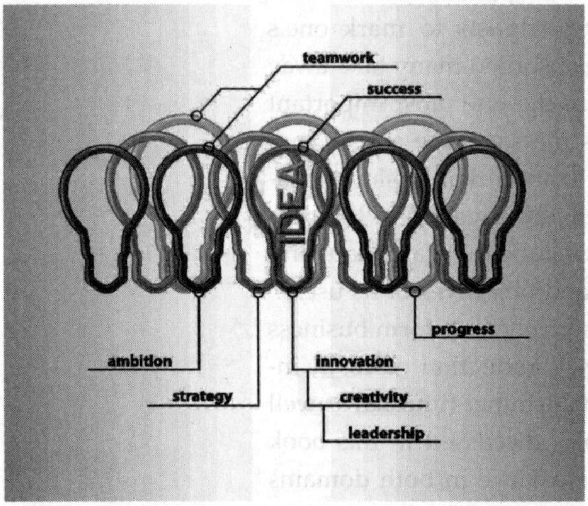

Bibliography

[1] S. Asur and B. A. Huberman. Predicting the future with social media. *IEEE/WIC/ACM International Conference on Web Intelligence and Intelligent Agent Technolgy*, pages 492–499, 2010.

[2] R. M. Bell, Y. Koren, and C. Volinsky. All together now: A perspective on the Netflix Prize. *Chance*, 23:24–29, 2010.

[3] Steven Bird, Ewan Klein, and Edward Loper. *Natural Language Processing with Python*. O'Reilly Media, 2009.

[4] Stephen Boyed and Lieven Vandenberghe. *Convex Optimization*. Cambridge University Press, 2004.

[5] Thomas H. Davenport and Jeanne G. Harris. *Competing on Analytics: The New Science of Winning*. Harvard Business School Press, 2007.

[6] Thomas H. Davenport, Jeanne G. Harris, and Robert Morison. *Analytics at Work: Smarter Decisions, Better Results*. Harvard Business School Press, 2010.

[7] S. Hill, F. Provost, and Volinsky C. Models of natural language understanding. In *Proceedings of the National Academy of Sciences of the United States of America*, volume 92, pages 9977–9982, 1995.

[8] S. Hill, F. Provost, and Volinsky C. Network-based marketing: Identifying likely adopters via consumer networks. *Statistical Science*, 21(2):256–276, 2006.

[9] Daniel Jurafsky and James H. Martin. *Speech and Language Processing, 2nd edition*. Pearson Prentice Hall, 2008.

[10] Estelle Marianne, Nick Merry, and Wendy Au. Customer experience modeling. In *SAS Global Forum 2012*, number 107-2012, 2012.

[11] Colleen McCue. *Data Mining and Predictive Analysis: Intelligence Gathering and Crime Analysis*. Butterworth-Heinemann, 2007.

[12] G. Miner, Dursun Delen, J. Elder, A. Fast, T. Hill, and R. A. Nisbet. *Practical Text Mining and Statistical Analysis for Non-Structured Text Data Applications*. Academic Press, Waltham, Mass., 2012.

[13] G. Oestreicher-Singer and A. Sundararajan. The visible hand of social networks in electronic markets. *Management Science*. Published online before print, June 15, 2012.

[14] R. T. Rockafellar. Lagrange multipliers and optimality. *SIAM Review*, 21(183), 1993.

[15] Christopher C. Shilakes and Julie Tylman. Enterprise Information Portals. *Merrill Lynch*, November 1998.

[16] G. Shmueli. *Practical Time Series Forecasting: A Hands-On Guide*. CreateSpace, 2nd edition, 2011.

[17] G. Shmueli. *Risk Analysis for Project Planning: A Hands-On Guide Using Excel*. CreateSpace, 2011.

[18] Galit Shmueli, Nitin R. Patel, and Peter C. Bruce. *Data Mining for Business Intelligence: Concepts, Techniques, and Applications in Microsoft Office Excel with XLMiner*. Wiley, 2010.

[19] Evan Stubbs. *Value of Business Analytics: Identifying the Path to Profitability*. Wiley, 2011.

[20] X. Su and T. M. Khoshgoftaar. A survey of collaborative filtering techniques. *Advances in Artificial Intelligence*, 2009.

[21] T. Ui. A note on discrete convexity and local optimality. *Japan J. Indust. Appl. Math.*, 23(21), 2006.

Index